The System of the Constitution

THE SYSTEM OF THE CONSTITUTION

Adrian Vermeule

OXFORD
UNIVERSITY PRESS

Oxford University Press, Inc., publishes works that further
Oxford University's objective of excellence
in research, scholarship, and education.

Oxford   New York
Auckland   Cape Town   Dar es Salaam   Hong Kong   Karachi
Kuala Lumpur   Madrid   Melbourne   Mexico City   Nairobi
New Delhi   Shanghai   Taipei   Toronto

With offices in
Argentina   Austria   Brazil   Chile   Czech Republic   France   Greece
Guatemala   Hungary   Italy   Japan   Poland   Portugal   Singapore
South Korea   Switzerland   Thailand   Turkey   Ukraine   Vietnam

Copyright © 2011 by Oxford University Press

Published by Oxford University Press, Inc.
198 Madison Avenue, New York, New York 10016

www.oup.com

Oxford is a registered trademark of Oxford University Press

Library of Congress Cataloging-in-Publication Data
Vermeule, Adrian.
    The system of the constitution / Adrian Vermeule.
        p.   cm.
        Includes bibliographical references and index.
        ISBN 978-0-19-983845-5 (alk. paper)
1. Constitutional law—United States.   2. System theory—United States.   I. Title.
    KF4550.V47   2011
    342.73—dc22   2011010001

CONTENTS

The System of the Constitution

Introduction: A System of Systems

his book attempts to trace out the ultimate implications of a single premise: any complex constitutional order, including our own, is best understood as a *system of systems*. The bare statement of the premise is delphic, but the idea is simple. Constitutional analysis examines the interaction among institutions, which are themselves equilibrium arrangements that result from the interaction of their individual members. So there are always two levels of aggregation in the picture: from individuals to institutions, and from institutions to an overall constitutional order. I use the term *systems* to designate such aggregates, whose properties are determined by the interaction of their components; those components may themselves be institutions as well as individuals. Hence constitutional orders are aggregates of aggregates—nested systems of systems.

For present purposes, the crucial feature of a system is that it may have emergent properties that differ from the properties of its components. Some examples:

- Even if all the members of a voting group have well-defined preferences, the group as a whole may have intransitive preferences, meaning that (in the simplest version) the group will choose A over B, B over C, and C over A. This sort of "preference cycling" makes the group's choice indeterminate and can yield arbitrary behavior; the group's choice may depend upon the order in which alternatives are presented to it, or the group may be unable to make any choice at all.

- In that example, the system effect arises when individual behavior is aggregated into group or institutional behavior. What happens when two such cycling institutions interact in an overall constitutional order? Counterintuitively, as we will see, the arbitrariness arising from intransitive group-level choices may actually be reduced, not exacerbated, by the interaction among component institutions all of whom are subject to preference cycling. The overall constitutional order can be less arbitrary than its components.

- If the constitutional order is democratic, somehow defined, it does not follow that each of the institutions that comprise it must itself be constituted in a democratic fashion. The overall order may be democratic only because one or more of its component institutions is designed to act in an undemocratic fashion, in order to check the self-destructive tendencies of democracy. The constitutional system may have a political property—democracy—that not all of its components share.

- Even if almost all judges are politically biased, it does not follow that a court will behave in a politically biased fashion. The judges' biases may be so distributed as to offset one another, leaving the few unbiased judges to cast decisive votes.

- Related to the last: Even if almost all judges on a court adopt a given approach to legal interpretation—for example, they are "originalists" who read the Constitution to track the original understanding of the founding generation—it does not follow that the court as whole will adopt the same approach. If the swing or marginal judge, who casts decisive votes, is not an originalist, the court as a whole will make nonoriginalist decisions.

In these examples, the aggregate system has properties that not all of its components or members share; as we will see, an aggregate system may even have properties that none of its components or members share. This is possible not because the aggregate has some mysterious existence of its own, over and above the individuals or institutions that comprise it. Rather it can occur just because the particular structure of interaction among the members or components produces emergent properties at the systemic level. As the examples also show, new properties can emerge either when individual interactions are aggregated into institutional behavior, or when institutional interactions are aggregated into the behavior of an overall constitutional order, or both. Constitutional orders, in other words, are two-level systems, and aggregation can produce surprises at either or both levels.

The possibility of such *system effects* is a stumbling block that has tripped up many constitutional theories, including both general theories of the constitutional order and partial theories addressed to particular parts of the constitutional order. So my critical thesis is that a great deal of constitutional theory and analysis goes wrong by overlooking that constitutional orders are two-level systems of this sort. Analysts uncritically assume that institutions must have the properties of their members, or that an overall constitutional order must have the properties of its component institutions. When they make mistakes of this sort, analysts make invalid claims about constitutional law and theory—invalid in the logical sense, such that the analysts' conclusions may or may not be true, but do not follow from their premises.

The systemic perspective on constitutionalism also yields constructive implications, addressed both to constitutional analysts and to the actors within the constitutional order. As for analysts, the implication is simply that an understanding of system effects enables not merely the avoidance of mistakes, but richer understanding. The systemic perspective brings into view new questions about how aggregation at multiple levels affects institutional behavior. It thereby marks out both a positive agenda for interdisciplinary work at the intersection of law and political science, and also a normative agenda for legal and political theory.

The positive questions are legion; here are a few examples, focusing solely on courts (other examples occur throughout the book). How does the ever-growing body of work on political biases in judging translate into the behavior of courts, given the possibility that judicial biases offset one another? Even if courts, as opposed to individual judges, act in a politically biased fashion, might judicial biases offset or counteract legislative biases, yielding a kind of political impartiality at the level of the overall lawmaking system? Do judges' approaches to constitutional law change as the composition of the court changes around them?

Normatively, the main question that a systemic perspective raises is whether we should evaluate constitutional orders piecemeal or wholesale. For example, suppose that many or most of the major lawmaking institutions of the constitutional order are undemocratic in one sense of that term, in that each of them partially frustrates the desires of a current majority. Suppose also, however, that these institutions depart from the democratic benchmark in different directions; each of them empowers different minorities, so that the overall constitutional order produces at the systemic level a kind of fair division of unfair political power, and thus a kind of second-order political equality. Is this system-level property normatively sufficient, or should we focus strictly on the retail normative objections to each institution, taken one by one? For political theory, this sort of question is largely unexplored terrain.

For actors within the constitutional order, the possibility of surprising system effects is ever-present. Actors who do not consider system effects may fail to anticipate perverse unintended consequences, and thus take self-defeating steps. As I will argue, for example, a judge ought not uncritically adopt the theory of judging that would be best if all (or a critical mass of) other judges were to adopt it. If the other judges do not do so, then the best approach to judging may change, even for the given judge. Judging, that is, is a systemically interdependent activity.

Awareness of system effects adds greatly to the uncertainty and complexity inherent in legal and political action. Here too, a systemic perspective marks out an agenda for the large swathe of legal theory that aims to guide officials in carrying out their assigned tasks. How should judges and nonjudicial officials behave so as to advance their aims, once they recognize the surprising system effects to which multimember bodies are subject? For example, how should judges committed to originalism decide cases in a world in which many other judges are not originalists, or not exclusively anyway? As we will see, the originalist judge in a world of nonoriginalist judges may do best, even by her own lights, to behave in a nonoriginalist fashion. As we will also see, however, under certain circumstances actors may do well to ignore the possibility of system effects, behaving as though they are oblivious or naive. This sort of highly sophisticated second-order naïveté may yield the same behavior as genuine first-order naïveté about system effects, yet the two approaches rest on very different approaches to decision making.

ANTECEDENTS: SYSTEMS THEORY AND LEGAL THEORY

The enterprise I have sketched draws upon a complex of related ideas: system effects, emergent properties, and the surprising consequences of aggregation, especially when multiple levels of aggregation are nested within one another. These ideas derive from a loosely related family of approaches called *systems theory*, variants of which can be found in fields as distant as computer science, biology, engineering, sociology, management, and organization theory.[1] Political scientists have made some use of systems theory,[2] but legal applications are few and far between.[3] A premise of the book is that systems theory, interpreted in pragmatic terms, is a natural and fitting tool for legal theory in general and constitutional theory in particular. Because legal systems are aggregates of aggregates—they arise from the interaction of institutions, which themselves arise in turn from the interaction of individuals—systems theory asks questions from which legal and constitutional theory can profit.

Systems theory is a sprawling, poorly integrated body of work; some of its applications reek of pseudoscience, as practitioners offer mysterious utterances about "complexity" and "chaos." Yet there is a core of genuine insight to systems theory that is not at all obscurantist or bogus. The core is the simple idea that institutions, groups and other aggregates—including nested aggregates of aggregates— can have emergent properties that cannot be deduced by inspecting their components or members in isolation, one by one.[4] Those properties arise from the interaction and relationship of the components. Although the system-level properties can be explained by reference to the behavior of the components, and are determined by that behavior, they are not reducible to that behavior; in the language of the philosophers, the system-level properties "supervene" upon the properties of the components, just as a shape composed of dots supervenes upon the position of the dots, without being reducible to them.[5]

The invalidity of attempts to reduce systems to their components gives rise to flabby talk about "reductionist Western science," and praise for "organicism" and "holism." Yet the core systems insight is entirely compatible with a rigorous version of methodological individualism, which can be defined for present purposes as the view—to which I emphatically subscribe—that the behavior of political and social groups is explicable, in principle, strictly by reference to the behavior of the individuals who make up those groups. The structure of interaction between individuals is itself what produces the emergent or supervening properties of the group.[6] But those properties need not be the same as the properties of the individuals, and as I will attempt to show, a good deal of legal theory falls flat because it overlooks that obstacle.

PLAN OF THE BOOK

Chapter 1 is illustrative, analytic, and methodological. I define system effects, provide a range of motivating examples, and describe two pitfalls into which analysts or actors can stumble when they overlook system effects. In the *fallacy of composition*, the mistake is to assume that if the components of an aggregate or members of a group have a certain property, the aggregate or group must also have that property. In the *fallacy of division*, the converse mistake is to assume that if the aggregate has a certain property, the components or members must have the same property. This chapter also clarifies the relationship between system effects and a famous idea in economics and political theory, the general theory of second best. Although the two ideas are conceptually distinct, they have close logical connections, and the theory of second best is a central problem both for actors within systems and for analysts of systems.

Chapter 2 turns from theory to application. I focus on the "structural constitution"—the design and composition of constitutional institutions and their interaction with other institutions. I attempt to show that systemic analysis improves our understanding of the design and composition of legislatures, the separation of powers, and judicial review, among other central topics. It also helps to identify a range of analytically invalid arguments about such topics, and thus produces a negative form of theoretical progress.

Constructively, a systemic approach to the structural constitution implies *second-best constitutionalism*. Suppose that at least some of the conditions necessary to produce a given ideal or first-best constitutional order fail to hold. Even if it would be best to achieve full satisfaction of all those conditions, it does not follow that it is best to achieve as many as possible of the conditions, taken one by one. Rather, multiple failures of the ideal can offset one other, producing a closer approximation to the ideal at the level of the overall system. Although the idea is abstract, it also turns out to be useful in many settings, or so I will try to show. Problems of the second best are chronic in real-world constitutional systems, including our own, because such systems are always partly constrained by technology, economics, and politics.

Chapters 3 and 4 focus on two crucial tools of systemic analysis that require extended treatment: *invisible-hand arguments* and *selection effects*. In chapter 3 the subject is invisible-hand arguments, which posit that the unintended by-product of individual or institutional interactions will produce some system-level good—welfare, truth, or justice, to name only a few of the possibilities. The relevant good emerges at the systemic level because of the interaction of individuals or institutions, who may be competing with one another or trading with one another, but who are not aiming to produce the system-level good and may not care whether or not it is produced. I outline the conditions under which such invisible-hand arguments can succeed or fail, critique some invisible-hand arguments that traditionally underpin American constitutional theory, and identify three critical and recurring dilemmas about such arguments. The overall goal is to delimit the valid scope of the invisible hand, which is a conceptually important genre of systemic reasoning, but which is often abused in legal, political, and economic theory.

In chapter 4 the subject is the selection of members of institutions, which themselves comprise the overall constitutional order. The traditional fodder of legal reasoning, and also of economic reasoning about law, is incentives: rules or policies that affect behavior by changing the costs and benefits of feasible actions. However, a recent wave of research in political science and economics has focused on selection, in which behavior is regulated not through incentives but by choosing individuals with the right preferences or beliefs (right from the selector's point of view). I will attempt to show that constitutional rules produce *systemic feedback effects* over time, via their indirect consequences on the selection of officeholders. Constitutional rules, that is, can change the pool of actual or potential officeholders in ways that either stabilize or destabilize the rules themselves. A systemic analysis of constitutional law must therefore take such effects into account. Whereas other chapters work with a synchronic definition of system effects, this chapter works with a diachronic one. Selection effects imply that, over time, changes in the membership of institutions may change the properties of the institutions themselves, and thereby change the overall constitutional order.

Chapter 5 turns from constitutional structure to the more traditional subject of constitutional theory: constitutional judging. My conclusions, however, are anything but traditional. The systemic approach implies that the choices of constitutional actors are strategically interdependent: the best course of action for any given constitutional actor will depend upon what other actors do. Judges deciding how to interpret statutes and the Constitution, for example, cannot simply assume, idealistically, that it would be best for them to adopt the approach that would be best for all if adopted by all. If others do not adopt that approach, then the nature of the best approach for the given judge may itself change, taking others' actions as nonideal constraints.

The implication, in other words, is *second-best legal interpretation*. A "textualist" judge who gives priority to the ordinary meaning of statutes and constitutional provisions must consider the possibility that it would be best, by her own lights, to be nontextualist in a world where many or most other judges are not textualist. Likewise, a judge who follows the approach outlined by the nineteenth-century legal scholar James Bradley Thayer, and who thus favors a regime of judicial deference to legislatures in matters of constitutional law, might decide that Thayerism is counterproductive if her colleagues are not Thayerian themselves. Even less intuitively, a judge who values systemic diversity within the judiciary may decide that it is best to be a textualist or a Thayerian precisely when, and because, most of her colleagues are not textualists or Thayerians.

The judge who takes system effects into account may thus change her approach in light of the behavior of her colleagues and the behavior of other institutions. Although such a judge is strategic, it does not follow that she is unprincipled. Rather, under identifiable conditions, the systemically minded judge will be a *strategic legalist* who attempts to act, within the constraints that arise from others' behavior, so as to nudge the legal system toward the best possible state, according to her view of the law. The strategic legalist is a consequentialist, but she attempts to maximize the quality of the law rather than the satisfaction of her own policy preferences.

Indeed, under identifiable conditions, the systemically minded judge may even be a kind of *legal chameleon*—a judge who changes her approach as the legal environment, including the behavior of other judges, changes around her, until the court as a whole reaches an equilibrium of optimal diversity. Such a course of action is psychologically demanding, probably too demanding to be pursued at the individual level. However, the systemic benefits that the legal chameleon creates can be attained at the systemic level instead. Wise appointments by presidents and senators aiming to diversify the judiciary would mimic, in a second-best way, the diversity that a bench of legal chameleons would produce. In these ways, and others I will attempt to identify, a systemic perspective puts new questions onto the agenda of constitutional and legal theory.

CHAPTER 1

Systemic Analysis

A system effect arises when the properties of an aggregate differ from the properties of its components or members, taken one by one.[1] In legal theory and the social sciences, the following are all familiar examples:

- Condorcet's voting paradox, in which the members of a collective choice group each have transitive preferences, yet group preferences are intransitive.[2]
- The "doctrinal paradox," in which logically consistent individual judgments over connected sets of propositions aggregate in such a way that the group's judgments are logically inconsistent.[3]
- The Prisoners' Dilemma, in which individually rational and self-interested behavior interacts so as to make all concerned worse off.[4]

Yet these examples are only the tip of the iceberg. The constitutional order is rife with system effects that are more important and less familiar. Although such effects are sometimes recognized in local contexts, they have a common analytic structure and can profitably be analyzed in global terms.

The failure to recognize system effects leads to fallacies of division and composition, in which the analyst mistakenly assumes that what is true of the aggregate must also be true of the members, or that what is true of the members must also be true of the aggregate.[5] Two examples I will explore at length, due to their importance for constitutional theory and legal theory more broadly, are (1) the fallacious assumption that if the overall constitutional order is to be democratic, each of its component institutions must be democratic, taken one by one; and (2) the fallacious assumption that if judges are politically biased, courts will issue politically biased rulings. In these cases, and many others I will discuss, system effects are an indispensable analytic tool.

SYSTEM EFFECTS: DEFINITION AND ILLUSTRATIONS

A definition. System effects arise either when what is true of the members of an aggregate is not true of the aggregate, or when what is true of the aggregate is not true of the members. The Condorcet Jury Theorem illustrates both possibilities. I will explore the theorem more fully below; a rough summary is that when (1) a group votes by majority rule on a binary choice, (2) one of the choices is defined as correct, according to the common fundamental preferences of the group's members, and (3) the competence (chance of being correct) of each member of the group is better than 0.5 (even if by a small margin), then the accuracy of the group will exceed that of the individual members, and will tend toward perfect accuracy as the size of the group increases. *The group may be more accurate than any of its individual members*, not because there is a mysterious group-level mind, but simply because the aggregation of individual judgments washes out random error, and thus produces greater accuracy at the level of the group—an emergent property. Accordingly, where a group votes on a binary choice under majority rule, and its average member is somewhat inaccurate, it is a fallacy of composition to assume that the group must be equally inaccurate. Conversely, the fallacy of division occurs when it is assumed that for the voting group to be highly accurate, its individual members must themselves be highly accurate, taken one by one.

In general, I will use the term *members* to denote the units whose behavior is aggregated to produce a system. In the analytically simplest cases, the members are people, and a system effect arises because the aggregate has different properties than do the individuals who compose it. Many of the most striking insights of the social sciences and legal theory have this structure. Well-known examples, which need be stated only in their simplest forms, include the following:

The invisible hand. In an invisible-hand mechanism, some kind of order or patterned outcome arises at the group level even if none of the individuals who comprise the group is attempting to create that order. The system-level pattern thus arises as the "result of human action, but not of human design."[6] As stated, the description is extremely general. The outcomes generated by the invisible hand may be benign or malign from the standpoint of the group involved, and also benign or malign from the standpoint of the wider society.

Starting with Bernard Mandeville's demonstration that private vices might aggregate and interact to create public virtues,[7] a central line of thought in economics and political economy has focused on *benign invisible-hand mechanisms,* especially market competition. Models of this sort are explicitly designed to dispel the belief that if none of the participants in the market is attempting to serve the public interest, the overall effects of the market must also be harmful to the public interest. Against this belief, Adam Smith offered his famous rejoinder:

> As every individual . . . by directing that industry in such a manner as its produce may be of the greatest value, he intends only his own gain, and he is in this, as in many other cases, led by an invisible hand to promote an end which was no part of his intention. . . . By pursuing his own interest he frequently promotes that of the society more effectually than when he really intends to promote it.[8]

As we will see, Madison attempted to transpose this major theme of the Scottish Enlightenment to the arena of constitutional design.

The logic of collective action. The flip side of Smith's argument is the *malign invisible-hand mechanism,* usually discussed under the rubric of collective action.[9] That each member of a group has an interest in a collective good does not mean the group will pursue that interest or produce that good, because of mutual free-riding. It is a straightforward fallacy of composition to assume that where each member would produce the good if acting alone, because the private benefits of doing so would exceed the private costs, it follows that all will do so if acting collectively, because the collective benefits exceed the collective costs. Conversely, it is a fallacy of division to assume that because the group has a collective interest in a given outcome, it must be in the interest of each member of the group to contribute their individual share to the collective good.[10]

The logic of collective action can yield overexploitation of public resources, as in the Tragedy of the Commons,[11] or else underproduction of public goods, including the public good of economic activity itself. In the "paradox of thrift," an attempt by each individual or family to save money perversely results in lower savings for all, because reduced economic activity lowers the income of each.[12] Here the fallacy of composition is to assume that if thrift benefits any given individual, thrift by all individuals must benefit the whole society.

The interest of any particular group may diverge from that of the wider society. A malign system-level outcome from the standpoint of the group may be a benign outcome from the standpoint of society, or vice versa. The inability of a producer cartel to cooperate in order to restrict output and raise prices above marginal cost, with a consequent reduction in overall social welfare, is a collective action problem from the standpoint of the cartel, but from the standpoint of society it is the benign working of the invisible hand. There is an analogous issue in the political domain. When, for example, legislators are unable to overcome the logic of collective action and cooperate on protecting legislative prerogatives, this outcome may be bad for legislators but may be bad, indifferent, or even positively desirable from the standpoint of social welfare.

Aggregation of preferences. The free-rider problem arises when decisions about how much to contribute to the collective interest are made individually, and are thus decentralized. One standard means for coping with the problems of collective action is to move from decentralized decision-making to collective choice, in which voting or some other aggregation mechanism is used to allow all concerned to make choices binding on all concerned. However, the move to genuinely collective choice does not obviate system effects.

A standard example, which I briefly introduced above, is Condorcet's voting paradox. Let us say that a *voting cycle* arises when three or more voters (1, 2, and 3) have preferences over three or more choices (A, B, and C), ordered as follows: voter 1 ranks the choices $A > B > C$, voter 2 ranks the choices $B > C > A$, and voter 3 ranks the choices $C > A > B$.[13] In pairwise voting under majority rule, A would beat B would beat C would beat A, by shifting majorities at each step. The consequence—the system effect—is that the group's collective preferences are intransitive although each individual's preferences are transitive. Because transitivity is often said to be a minimum necessary condition of rationality, one might then see the group's preference ordering as being irrational despite the assumed rationality of all members of the group. This personifies the group, however, so a less freighted description of the problem is just that the group's *choice* is indeterminate under majority rule. In particular, an agenda setter can determine which result will be chosen by ordering the votes in a particular sequence and then applying an arbitrary stopping rule.[14]

Condorcet's voting paradox was later generalized into Arrow's Theorem, which holds that for at least three voters and three choices, there is no collective choice mechanism that can simultaneously satisfy a minimal list of desiderata: very roughly, it should not make any individual a dictator, should be universal in the sense that it admits any preference ordering by any voter and uses all the orderings to generate a determinate social choice, should ignore alternatives that are not before the group, and should prefer a certain option if every member of the group does so.[15] Arrow's theorem has generated an impossibly large literature that refines its conditions and considers the consequences of varying one or all of them.[16] For my purposes, however, Condorcet's original paradox suffices to bring out the system effects of preference aggregation and the important idea of preference cycles, so I need not explore the generalized version here.

Aggregation of beliefs and judgments. Condorcet's paradox arises among voters with different fundamental preferences. However, system effects may also arise among voters with different factual beliefs or normative judgments (and hence different derived preferences over choices). Three examples are especially useful: the miracle of aggregation, the Condorcet Jury Theorem, and the "doctrinal paradox" or "discursive dilemma."

The miracle of aggregation. Under political democracy, even if almost all voters are ignorant or biased, it is a fallacy of composition to assume that the electorate as a whole must necessarily act as though ignorant or biased. Lord Bryce, anticipating a large literature by more than half a century, observed that

> the educated and reflective class in America…may be numerically a small minority of the voters, but as in many states the two regular parties command a nearly equal normal voting strength, a small section detached from either party can turn an election by throwing its vote for the candidate, to whichever party he belongs, whom it thinks capable and honest. Thus a comparatively independent group wields a power in elections altogether disproportionate to its numbers.[17]

Analytically, this so-called "miracle of aggregation" means that the collective choice of an electorate might be far superior to the choices of most of the voters in the collective, *if* those voters' mistakes are distributed in the right way.[18] Suppose an election between two candidates, *A* and *B*, and an electorate of 100. Suppose also that *A* is a much better candidate than *B* (however "better" is defined), but that 98 percent of the electorate are blind partisans who ignore the quality of the candidates. Of the 98 percent, half are blind *A*-partisans who will vote for *A* no matter what, and half are blind *B*-partisans who will vote for *B* no matter what. Fortunately, however, the remaining 2 percent of the electorate are highly informed independents who care only about the quality of candidates, not their party, and thus vote for the better candidate with 100% probability. Candidate *A* wins by a vote of 51–49. The electorate as a whole is certain to pick the better candidate even though 98 percent of voters are maximally biased, because the biases of the 98 percent offset one another.

The miracle is powered by a statistical trick or principle, the law of large numbers: as the size of a sample group increases, the expected frequency of an event and the actual frequency will tend to converge.[19]

Suppose that the 98 percent are not blind partisans, but vote randomly, perhaps by flipping a fair coin. The larger the number of voters, the more likely it is that the coin flips converge to an even split, 49 percent to 49 percent. When the convergence is sufficiently close, exactly the same result holds as in the case of the biased voters, and the miracle goes through.

Condorcet's Jury Theorem. Given its basis in the law of large numbers, the miracle of aggregation is a mathematical relative of the Jury Theorem, which is also powered by the law. We have already seen that in the simplest possible form, the theorem states that where a group votes sincerely on two alternatives, one of which is correct, and the members of the group are even slightly more likely to be right than wrong, then as the number of members in the group increases, the probability that a majority vote of the group is correct tends toward certainty.[20] Although the theorem can be extended in many directions, the only one I will mention is that it can hold if the members of the group have dissimilar chances of getting the answer right, so long as the mean competence is better than random.[21]

The system effect here is that a majority of the group will, given the other conditions of the theorem, necessarily prove more competent than the average individual and perhaps even more competent than the most competent individual. The other edge of the sword is that if the group's average competence is lower than random, the same amplification occurs in the other direction, and the performance of the group tends downward.[22] In either case, it is fallacious to assume that smart (dumb) groups must have equally smart (dumb) members. Group performance diverges from the performance of (average) individuals.

Importantly, it is also a fallacy of division to assume that unbiased groups must have unbiased members. One of the principal surprises of the theorem is that the degree to which members' errors are correlated is as important to group performance as is group competence.[23] So long as the biases of group members are uncorrelated or negatively correlated and thus point in different directions, they will tend to wash out in the aggregate.[24] This is, of course, the miracle of aggregation; as we will see, this possibility undermines the large recent literature on the political biases of judges on multimember courts.[25]

The doctrinal paradox or discursive dilemma. While the miracle of aggregation and the Jury Theorem address the ability of groups to produce correct answers, a separate issue involves the ability of groups to achieve coherent answers. In the "doctrinal paradox"[26] or "discursive dilemma,"[27] a group whose members' judgments are coherent in the minimal sense of logical consistency may not display logical consistency at the group level. Consider the profile of judgments on the truth of propositions p and q and the conditional "If p then q" shown in table 1.1.

Just as shifting majorities may cause preference cycling, so too they may cause the group to hold illogical collective judgments even if all the group's members are entirely logical. Here too, however, a less provocative way of stating the problem is in terms of indeterminacy rather than incoherence: a given profile of judgments will yield different collective judgments under different aggregation procedures.

Table 1.1 A MAJORITARIAN INCONSISTENCY

	p	"If p then q"	q
Individual 1	True	True	True
Individual 2	True	False	False
Individual 3	False	True	False
Majority	True	True	False

Source: Christian List, *Collective Wisdom: Lessons from the Theory of Judgment Aggregation*, table 2, available at http://personal.lse.ac.uk/LIST/pdf-files/Collective Wisdom19Oct.pdf.

Given the foregoing profile of judgments, for example, there is an important choice between two procedures: (1) a direct majority-rule vote on the truth of q; (2) a premise-based procedure that takes majority votes on p and on "If p then q" and then automatically determines that the conclusion q is true if a majority approves of both premises. The first procedure yields a group judgment that q is false, the second that it is true.

Standard illustrations of the doctrinal paradox involve majority rule in courts, where the paradox was originally developed.[28] However, nothing inherent in the logic of the problem is restricted to (1) majority rule, (2) doctrinal judgments as opposed to other sorts of judgments, or (3) courts as opposed to other institutions. A general impossibility result, comparable to Arrow's Theorem, shows that no aggregation procedure can guarantee collective coherence while satisfying a list of attractively minimal criteria.[29] Moreover, even within courts, the logic of the problem can be generalized from judgments about outcomes in particular cases to judgments about the rules of law that should be used to generate those outcomes.[30] This "generalized doctrinal paradox"[31] is important but largely unexplored terrain.

MEMBERS: INDIVIDUALS, INSTITUTIONS, OR PROPOSITIONS

In the previous examples, the members of the aggregate were people, while the aggregates were groups of people. But nothing requires this. In many of the most interesting cases for public law, the members are themselves institutions, and institutions then aggregate to form an overall constitutional system. As I will discuss shortly, this implies a two-level system: individuals form an institutional system, and institutions form a constitutional system—an overall constitutional order.

Alternatively, the units of the system might be neither individuals nor institutions. Instead they might be propositions of fact, morality, or law. A set of legal provisions may have properties that differ from the properties of some or all of its individual members, just as a collection of letters may have an emergent meaning that constitutes a word, even if none of the word's component letters is itself a word.

Here is an extended example, in which a set of legal claims or propositions displays emergent properties.

The (ir)relevance of constitutional amendments. David Strauss has argued that constitutional amendments are "irrelevant" because an amendment is neither a necessary nor a sufficient condition for legal change. His core irrelevance thesis holds as follows:

> [S]ubject to only a few qualifications, our system would look the same today if Article V of the Constitution had never been adopted and the Constitution contained no provision for formal amendment.[32]

For present purposes, the important feature of this argument is that it slips imperceptibly from the denial that *any particular* amendment is relevant to the denial that the *total set* of amendments is relevant. In many cases, as we will see, the argument establishes the irrelevance of particular amendments only by pointing to other amendments which would otherwise have subsumed the functions of the irrelevant amendment. But if the reason that particular amendments are irrelevant is that other amendments would have been interpreted to produce the same effect, then the irrelevance claim cannot hold true of all amendments at once.

To illustrate the problem, consider Strauss's argument that the protracted struggles over the rejected Equal Rights Amendment, which would have constitutionalized a guarantee of gender equality, were irrelevant. "Today, it is difficult to identify any respect in which constitutional law is different from what it would have been if the ERA [the Equal Rights Amendment] had been adopted."[33] The point is that the Supreme Court subsequently read a strong presumption against gender discrimination into the Fourteenth Amendment's Equal Protection Clause.[34] The ERA was irrelevant because the work it would otherwise have done was picked up by (the Court's reading of) a different constitutional amendment.

If that is so, however, then the ERA was or would have been irrelevant only because there was a different amendment in the picture that picked up the slack, and which must therefore have itself been relevant. To be sure, the Court's decision to interpret equal protection in this way was necessary for this story; but it is equally true that the Court felt it necessary to find some text, somewhere in the picture, into which gender equality could be read. Absent the Equal Protection Clause, the Court might have used some other text—say, the Privileges and Immunities Clause[35]—but then that text would have been relevant in turn.

Strauss's irrelevance argument takes a similar form in many cases, although the structure of the argument is often tacit rather than explicit. Here are some examples:

- As previously described, the ERA was irrelevant because its content was subsumed in the Equal Protection Clause of the Fourteenth Amendment.[36]
- In similar vein, had the Nineteenth Amendment not been enacted, "the nation's commitment to women's suffrage would have been just as profound . . . an influence on the interpretation of the Equal Protection Clause."[37]
- An omitted provision of the Twenty-fourth Amendment, which would have abolished poll taxes in state elections, was "adopted" by the Court through interpretation of the Equal Protection Clause.[38]

- Absent the Fourteenth Amendment, the effects of the Equal Protection Clause on state-sponsored segregation would have been achieved through interpretation of the Due Process Clause of the Fifth Amendment, the Guaranty Clause of Article I, or some other text.[39]
- The proposed Child Labor Amendment was irrelevant because the Supreme Court expanded the Commerce Clause to achieve the same results.[40]

The underlying problem may be illustrated schematically by imagining a set of twenty-six constitutional amendments. For any amendment A in the set, we might argue that A's functions would have been subsumed by some other member of the set, say B; B's functions would have been subsumed by C; and so on, the final claim being that the only amendment not yet shown to be irrelevant, Z, would in turn have been subsumed by A. Arguing piecemeal in this way, we can then proceed to examine each amendment seriatim and show that it is irrelevant. What results is a series of individually plausible arguments that *any particular* amendment is irrelevant. However, the series cannot be generalized to claim that the whole *set* of amendments is irrelevant simultaneously. To show that any given amendment is irrelevant through the seriatim procedure, we cannot help but posit that some other amendment in the set is relevant, although the identity of the relevant amendment changes at each step in the argument.

Even if every particular constitutional amendment can be shown to be irrelevant through a seriatim procedure, it is a fallacy of composition to conclude that all constitutional amendments might be irrelevant simultaneously. At least one amendment must be in place and be efficacious in order to subsume the others. Indeed, the generalization may not hold even if all of the constituent claims are each plausible, taken one by one. This is a system effect, arising from the aggregation of a group of legal propositions rather than a group of individuals or a group of institutions.

TWO-LEVEL SYSTEMS

So far the discussion has been confined to one-level systems, in which the relevant aggregate is composed of either individuals or legal propositions. However, many of the cases of greatest interest to constitutional theory involve *two-level systems*. Institutions are systems that aggregate the desires, beliefs, and choices of individuals, and those institutions may have very different properties than do the individuals who compose them. Furthermore, the interaction among institutions itself creates a system at the second level, one which may have very different properties than the institutions that compose it. Hence constitutionalism is a system of systems. System effects can arise at the first level, the aggregation of individual properties into institutional outcomes; at the second level, the aggregation of institutional properties into an overall constitutional order; or at both levels, with complex interactions.

To illustrate, I will elaborate an example I introduced above. Drawing on the Condorcet voting paradox and its generalization in Arrow's Theorem, public choice theorists developed models of preference cycling and applied them to legislatures and courts. As to courts, it was shown that the Supreme Court might in principle rule intransitively, favoring legal claim A over B over C over A, even though all of the Court's members had transitive preferences.[41] Even if the cycle remained implicit and thus not actually observed, the need for an arbitrary stopping rule would render the outcome highly sensitive to the order in which cases arose, and would thus give great power to whoever sets the Court's agenda.[42]

Roughly simultaneously, libertarian critics of democracy invoked Arrow's Theorem to impeach the outputs of legislatures, arguing that the same phenomena of implicit but unavoidable cycles, arbitrary stopping rules, path-dependence, and agenda control cut the link between legislative inputs—the preferences of the legislators—and the statutes that legislatures produce, and thus severed the transmission belt of representative democracy. Theorists of this stripe advocated reducing the scope of government and transferring power to the courts.[43]

In both cases, theorists pointed to system effects arising when individual preferences are aggregated into institutional decisions. Both sets of analysts were, quite correctly, exposing a traditional fallacy of composition: the assumption, common to both traditional legal theory and to traditional democratic theory, that well-behaved preferences on the part of individual members of legislatures or courts would translate into well-behaved collective decision-making. However, putting the two results together created a conundrum. If the model of preference cycling applied just as much to courts as to legislatures, then the arbitrariness of legislation would be compounded, or at least would not be improved, by the arbitrariness of courts.[44]

This conundrum turned out to be illusory, once it was observed that cycling in *both* institutions might result in less, not more, cycling in the system overall.[45] In a lawmaking system composed of both legislatures and courts, cycles triggered by different circumstances in the two institutions might offset one another, resulting in less arbitrariness at the level of the system than at the level of any of the component institutions, taken one by one. Here the fallacy of composition is the assumption that if two institutions cycle, their interaction in a system of joint lawmaking must display all the more instability and arbitrariness.[46]

Analogously, an important defense of legislative bicameralism is that dividing the legislature into two parts may reduce the ability of agenda setters to exploit majority cycles.[47] Because "the agenda setter's best strategy is to manipulate the order of consideration so that the preferred alternative is considered later rather than earlier, to the extent that a second chamber begins deliberation by considering the other chamber's proposal, the first chamber's agenda setter...will be at the mercy of the order of consideration in the other chamber."[48] This argument points to offsetting cycles in different chambers of the legislature, rather than in different branches of government, but the two ideas are structurally parallel.

Although in these examples the first-level and second-level system effects were discovered in chronological sequence, a two-level system can be decomposed into distinct analytic steps, in whatever historical fashion those steps are discovered or taken. First, the primitives of the system, here individuals, are aggregated into an institution, whose properties may or may not track the properties of its components. Second, at least two such institutions form a system, whose properties may or may not track the properties of its components. As the development of cycling theory in public law indicates, system effects at either or both levels may produce highly counterintuitive results.

SYSTEM EFFECTS AND THE SECOND BEST

The possibility of offsetting cycles in legislatures and courts, or in two branches of a legislature, exemplifies a larger phenomenon with close analytic connections to the logic of system effects: the *general theory of second best*.[49] The theory holds that where it is not possible to satisfy all the conditions necessary for an economic system to reach an overall optimum, it is not generally desirable to satisfy as many of those conditions as possible.[50] Rather, the failure to satisfy optimality conditions on one variable means that other variables must take on suboptimal values as well, in order to compensate for the initial failure.[51] The idea can apply to a part or sector of the economic system as well as to the whole. It is desirable that a given industry be both competitive and nonpolluting, but if excessive pollution is inevitable, then a monopoly might be best; competition would increase the number of firms and make pollution even worse, inflicting harm that could exceed the increased consumer surplus from competition.[52]

The logical connection between the general theory of second best and the idea of system effects is that the theory explains the consequences of systemic interaction among multiple institutional variables. It is tempting to think that if it would be best for *all* variables in an institutional system to take on their optimal values, then it would be best for *each* variable to take on its optimal value, considering the variables one by one.[53] The general theory of second best, however, exposes this idea as a fallacy of division. Because the variables interact, a failure to attain the optimum in the case of one variable will necessarily affect the optimal value of the other variables. Conversely, even if some or even all the variables in the system take on suboptimal or nonideal values, it is a fallacy of composition to think that the system overall must be suboptimal or nonideal. The interaction between several nonideal elements can produce an overall system that is as close as possible to the ideal.

The second best in politics and law. Originally developed in economics, the general theory of second best generalizes easily to any legal or political theory that takes the consequences of legal structures or policy choices into account.[54]

- Discussing the unwritten "mixed" constitution of the Roman Republic, Polybius argued that its long-term equilibrium arose from offsetting departures from the political ideal: the excessive power of the consuls was balanced by the Senate's ability to use corrupt means, such as government contracts, to ensure the dependence and adherence of the people.[55]

- Alexis de Tocqueville argued that the uncheckable power of the French monarchy before 1789 was hobbled by the monarch's own greed: the Crown sold so many offices that it had to channel its administrative decrees through a highly inefficient bureaucracy.[56] A similar idea has been applied to many other systems: both the Russia of the tsars and the indigenous monarchies of India have been described as "despotism tempered by corruption."[57]

- In a counterpoint to Polybius and Tocqueville, David Hume explained the balance of the unwritten British constitution as a by-product of executive corruption. Although the power of Parliament had swelled beyond all control after 1688, the Crown managed to maintain the balance by exploiting collective action problems among legislators, offering government sinecures and other forms of bribery to induce a decisive bloc of legislators to sell their votes on the cheap.[58] I explain these divide-and-conquer tactics in more detail below.

- Hume also argued that the first-best constitutional design would contain, inter alia, an executive who was (1) elected at (2) regular intervals. However, Hume continued, suppose that some political constraint mandated that the executive must serve for life. In that case, the second best would be a hereditary monarch rather than what is, in effect, an elected monarch. "[A] crown is too high a reward ever to be given to merit alone, and will always induce the candidates to employ force, or money, or intrigue, to procure the votes of the electors."[59]

- Bernard Mandeville suggested that the excessive mutability of the laws, which change at the same rate as fashions, compensates for the inability of legislators to anticipate the problems of the future.[60] The first-best regime would have laws that are both perfectly farsighted and enduring; given the inevitable limits of legislative foresight, however, the second-best regime both enacts myopic laws and quickly alters them.

- Commenting on the elaborate technical rules governing criminal indictments at English common law, Sir James Fitzjames Stephen argued that although the rules were farcical in themselves, "they did mitigate, though in an irrational, capricious manner, the excessive severity of the old criminal law."[61]

- Theorists of deliberative democracy argue that an appeal to self-interest or an exercise of coercive power can be legitimate when, and because, others are appealing to their self-interest or exercising their power coercively. Although the first-best would involve impartial deliberation by all, when some violate the obligation of impartiality, others may follow suit in order to "produce[] as close as possible an approximation to the ideal of no power in the deliberation."[62]

The application of the theory of second best to written constitutions is straightforward. In principle, constitutions are package solutions that must be evaluated and reformed as total systems. In reality, short of a revolutionary situation, some parts of any constitution are fixed at any given time, and even after revolutionary situations, constitutional designers face political and economic constraints which mandate or exclude certain constitutional features.

Here are some brief examples of second-best arguments in American constitutional theory, from the many that could be chosen (and I will explore other examples in the later discussion):

- It has been argued that the first-best understanding of the American Constitution would prohibit both delegation of excessive authority to the president and also the legislative veto. However, "a world with both delegations and legislative vetoes is closer to the correct constitutional 'baseline' than is a world with only delegations."[63] Similar arguments have been made for other checks on delegated authority.[64]

- Suppose that the constitutional first-best would be a lawmaking system in which Congress rolls no logs and the executive is put to the choice of either vetoing or approving bills as a whole. Suppose also, however, that congressional logrolling and omnibus legislation are ineradicable; instead or in addition, suppose that collective action problems within Congress cause legislators to enact more pork-barrel spending than even legislators themselves would want. In such cases, the president's veto power might be interpreted, on strictly functional grounds, as authorizing a line-item veto—a form of compensating adjustment that approximates the first-best regime.[65]

- If the constitutional first-best is a parliamentary system with proportional representation, it does not follow that proportional representation is still desirable in a system with an independently elected executive. The risk in such a system is that a powerful president will dominate a legislature fractured among many small parties.[66] A first-past-the-post electoral system, whatever its intrinsic defects, might be desirable for its tendency to produce two consolidated major parties,[67] which can more successfully resist executive encroachments.

- James Landis argued that independent administrative agencies were a compensating adjustment that offset the power of the presidency, restoring something like the original Madisonian system of checks and balances in a world where legislative and judicial checks on the executive proved inadequate. "[P]aradoxically enough, though [the creation of administrative power] may seem in theoretic violation of the doctrine of the separation of power, it may in matter of fact be the means for the preservation of the content of that doctrine."[68]

- The converse of Landis's argument is the claim that the Constitution should be read to establish a "unitary executive," even though originally it did not.[69] On this view, a departure from the original understanding is necessary because administrative business is more political and less technical today than it was in the founding era; the unitary executive is an adjustment designed to ensure that a politically accountable official, the president, can oversee the discretionary action of the bureaucracy in a highly politicized world.[70]

- It can be argued that although judicial review would be desirable in a system of mutual checks and balances between legislature and judiciary, it would be undesirable if the power of the judiciary were essentially unchecked.[71] In such a case, legislative supremacy over constitutional matters might be the second best.

- Suppose that government officials have incentives to classify too much information, in part because they do not bear the full costs to democratic government of doing so. Suppose also, however, that journalists have incentives to report too much classified information, in part because they do not bear the full costs to national security of doing so. Under optimistic assumptions, these two sets of skewed incentives create an "unruly contest"[72] between officials and journalists that might produce a socially optimal level of disclosure overall.[73]

- Suppose that the first-best system of criminal procedure would be inquisitorial, with a well-informed magistrate playing the roles of prosecutor, judge, and jury. However, given positive information costs, which may be relatively higher for magistrates than for the parties themselves, the second best might be an adversarial system of procedure. Although no party will be motivated to seek and produce the whole truth, competition between parties with private information may produce more total information than a poorly informed magistrate could obtain, and may thus yield the closest possible approximation to truth overall.[74]

- As I will discuss at length in chapter 5, second-best arguments can also apply to judicial interpretation of written constitutions. Justice Antonin Scalia initially argued for originalism on second-best rather than first-best grounds: even if the first-best interpretive regime would license judges to update constitutional law as circumstances change, judges would systematically err by imposing current values too frequently.[75] Originalism creates a drag on this tendency, resulting in a closer approximation to an optimal rate of judicial updating. Originalism is thus akin to "the librarian who talks too softly."[76]

- An important special case of second-best constitutionalism is translation theory—the idea that as circumstances change, the original meaning of the Constitution's structure might best be preserved by departures from the specific original understandings of the founding generation.[77] On this view, "to be faithful to the constitutional structure, the Court must be willing to be unfaithful to the constitutional text."[78] Translation is a special case along two dimensions: it is addressed to constitutional interpreters, rather than constitutional designers, and it is best understood as a version of purposivism that tries to map original understandings onto changed circumstances by boosting the level of generality at which those understandings are defined.

Having provided definitions and motivating examples, I will try to mark the limitations of systemic analysis, so as not to promise too much. In all of these examples, and others I will introduce in the following chapters, systemic reasoning is essential and, I hope, illuminating. Yet I do not claim that systemic analysis can, all by itself, underwrite substantive conclusions about any of the questions or problems I shall discuss. Alertness to the fallacies of composition and division can tell us whether an argument is valid, but not whether its conclusions are true. What systemic analysis can provide is a series of possibility theorems, intended to show that system effects are analytically inescapable[79] and that many standard problems must be analyzed in different terms once latent system effects are brought to the surface. A major source of analytic confusion is that constitutional law is a system of systems, which means that constitutional analysts must take account of the complexities and counterintuitive possibilities inherent in two-level systems.

This analytic enterprise does not depend upon the normative theory that is used to evaluate constitutional and legal rules. In the arguments I will examine in succeeding chapters, the first-best criterion for evaluating rules may be overall welfare, or instead satisfaction of the preferences of current majorities, or instead some more complex conception of democracy, all of which may have different implications in different cases. In any given setting I will attempt to specify clearly which first-best criterion is in play, but my aim is precisely not to choose among those theories. Rather, it is to show that system effects and problems of second best are ubiquitous and are not theory-dependent.

Finally, the claim that system effects are inescapable for the constitutional *analyst* does not imply that they will or must always be considered by constitutional *actors* within the system. As I will illustrate throughout, constitutional actors may sometimes decide that the complexity, uncertainty, and strategic indeterminacy inherent in a systemic perspective create burdens of judgment or decision costs so great that it is best to behave as though the actor exists in splendid isolation, rather than within a larger interdependent system. I believe that this form of sophisticated naïveté is very different than the genuine naïveté of the actor who is oblivious to system effects, even if the resulting behavior is observationally equivalent; the two actors take different stances toward system effects and do not use the same decision rules to choose their common behavior. In any event, sophisticated naïveté about system effects stems from the decision costs facing constitutional actors who must act in real time with limited information, unlike external analysts of the constitutional order, whose goal is understanding rather than action. The constitutional analyst thus has no warrant for naïveté, whether sophisticated or simpleminded.

CHAPTER 2

The Structural Constitution

I turn now to applications of systemic reasoning. This chapter examines system effects that arise from the constitutional structure. I will attempt to show that structural constitutional law is rife with system effects, and that such effects have been overlooked in many standard accounts of constitutional theory and legal theory generally.[1]

CHECKS, BALANCES, AND THE INVISIBLE HAND

I begin with what may be James Madison's most famous idea in constitutional theory, the idea in *The Federalist No. 51* that

> the great security against a gradual concentration of the several powers in the same department consists in giving to those who administer each department the necessary constitutional means and personal motives to resist encroachments of the others. The provision for defence

must in this, as in all other cases, be made commensurate to the danger of attack. Ambition must be made to counteract ambition.[2]

Madison is best understood to offer here a *benign invisible-hand account of checks and balances*, one heavily influenced by the general ideas of the Scottish Enlightenment,[3] whose major figures—Adam Ferguson, David Hume, and Adam Smith—all employed benign invisible-hand reasoning in more or less detailed forms.[4] I will detail the analytic structure of invisible-hand arguments in chapter 3; for now, I will examine the implications of such arguments for checks and balances and the separation of powers, cornerstones of the American constitutional order.

Madison's basic idea in the domain of constitutional design has the same structure as Smith's basic idea in the domain of political economy.[5] Just as it is fallacious to think that the market can only promote the public interest, somehow defined, if its participants aim to benefit the public, so too it is a fallacy of division to think that the public interest somehow defined can only be attained, in a system of separated powers, if each of the component institutions itself aims to promote the public interest. Madison offers what is in substance, and almost in terms, a second best argument. The first best would be to have governing officials who are motivated to pursue the public interest: "If angels were to govern men, neither external nor internal controls on government would be necessary."[6] Failing this, the second best is to ensure an array of institutions, each of which promotes its own institutional ambitions.

As the theory of second best indicates, however, if universal pub-lic-spiritedness is ruled out, it would not necessarily be desirable to approach as close as possible to the institutional ideal of public-spirited motivation. It is at best unclear whether the Madisonian system would work as intended if some, but not all, of the institutions in the system promote the public interest while others solely pursue their institutional ambitions. In the worst possible case, public-spirited officials in (say) the legislature would consider both the legitimate institutional interests of the legislature and the legitimate institutional interests of the executive, while executive officials strictly interested in aggrandizing executive power would consider only their own institutional interests. The interests of the executive would then be double-counted.

To avoid this malign dynamic, it is not necessary that *all* institutions act to promote their institutional ambitions. If, say, the president and the Congress are relentlessly self-promoting as institutions, while the Court decides on the merits of particular cases, then the ambitions of the first two institutions may cancel each other out, allowing the public interest to emerge. The general theory of second best does not entail that lack of universal public-spiritedness must necessarily yield bad results, only that it can do so. (This example is structurally analogous to the miracle of aggregation, discussed in chapter 1.) Yet the larger point remains: Madison's systemic paradox, whose radicalism often goes unappreciated, is that the invisible hand of checks and balances requires multiple and offsetting institutional ambitions in order to mimic the first-best case of universal public-spiritedness. Structurally similar puzzles arise in many other legal contexts in which invisible-hand reasoning is invoked, and I will examine them in detail in chapter 3.

Despite its paradoxical appeal, there are two analytic flaws in the Madisonian argument. To identify these flaws, we must note that the argument implicitly has a two-level systemic structure. First, the ambitions of individual officials must be aggregated within the separate institutions they staff so as to promote the ambitions or interests of those institutions. Second, the institutions must interact in such a fashion that, by each institution promoting its own ambition, the overall optimum of checks and balances is attained. Madison's argument is vulnerable at both levels.

As to the first level, in which individual ambitions are aggregated into institutional behavior, nothing guarantees that the interests of individual officials will be aligned with the institutional ambitions or interests of the institutions they staff.[7] Madison seems to have assumed, casually, that the structure of lawmaking institutions would suffice to ensure that "[t]he interest of the man" is "connected with the constitutional rights of the place."[8] However, the individual ambitions or interests of the members of institutions might not aggregate so as to ensure that the institution pursues its interests, however such interests are defined. At this level Madison implicitly fell prey to the fallacy of composition by supposing that the pursuit of individual ambitions by officials would ensure the pursuit of institutional ambition at the institutional level.[9] Madison in essence overlooked the logic of collective action, assuming instead that within a given institution each official would do what is in the interest of all.

There are two possible responses to this critique. First, mechanisms of psychological identification might align individual and institutional interests, under particular conditions.[10] But those mechanisms must be specified and investigated in particular cases; their existence cannot be assumed. Another response is the second best possibility that *divergences between individual and institutional interests across branches might offset one another.* If individual legislators have imperfect incentives to promote the institutional interests of Congress, and if the same is true of individual presidents and judges for their respective branches, then the overall result of the system of imperfect competition might approximate the same equilibrium of power that would arise if individual and branch incentives were perfectly aligned in all institutions.

To bracket the foregoing issues, let us assume a perfect alignment between individual and institutional interests. Even in that case,

Madison's argument is still vulnerable at the second level of interaction *among* institutions. The argument lacks any mechanism to ensure that competition among institutions promoting their interests or ambitions will promote either a state of affairs or a dynamic process that is desirable overall, such as optimal mutual checking by government institutions. Institutions will bear costs and enjoy benefits from checking the ambitions of other institutions, costs and benefits that will vary with the contingencies of politics. But there is nothing that necessarily or systematically aligns the institutional costs and benefits with social costs and benefits. Madisonian institutional competition might for all we know produce too little mutual checking or too much, and if it happened to produce optimal checks somehow defined, that would be merely a happy coincidence, not likely to remain stable over the long run.

At both levels of aggregation, the common problem is that there is no valid analogy to the case of markets. Adam Smith's benign invisible-hand argument, that self-interested behavior in the market would create public benefits,[11] was later elaborated and shown to rest on a well-specified mechanism: the price system, which in principle ensures allocative and productive efficiency in perfectly competitive markets and in that sense aligns individual and social interests. By contrast, there is no robust mechanism, analogous to prices, that could even in principle align the individual ambitions of officials with the interests of the institutions they staff, or align the interaction of institutions with the public interest somehow defined. Madison thus offers an *ersatz invisible-hand argument,* one that has the form but not the substance of Smith's.[12]

This point is missed by modern scholars who describe the separation of powers as a system of "spontaneous order."[13] Absent a regulating mechanism such as the price system, the separation of powers is certainly decentralized, but it need not generate any kind of patterned order, let alone a socially beneficial one. Rather it will produce haphazard results that vary with the contingencies of politics. Spontaneous orders arise as a result of decentralized interactions in a system, but not all decentralized interactions in a system result in spontaneous orders, let alone benign ones.

THE LEGISLATURE AND THE EXECUTIVE

In many cases, the interaction between the executive and legislature, or between the chambers of a legislature, tends to produce problems of composition and division, because of the collective character of legislatures (at the first level of aggregation) and because of the system effects of institutional interactions (at the second level of aggregation).

Vote-buying and the divide-and-conquer strategy.[14] As indicated above, Hume argued that although Parliament taken as a collective body was far stronger than the Crown, the Crown could maintain itself by divide-and-conquer tactics, especially vote-buying and corruption that exploited collective action problems among the members.[15] "[T]he interest of the body is here restrained by that of the individuals.... [T]he house of commons stretches not its power, because such an usurpation would be contrary to the interest of the majority of its members."[16] Although Hume is vague on the details, we may interpret the story according to modern economic models of the externalities involved in vote-selling.

Two interpretations are possible. In the first,[17] the Crown offers a cheap bribe to each legislator for voting in its favor. Suppose there is a private cost to each legislator of voting with the Crown when other legislators do not; perhaps the legislator is then conspicuously exposed to the slings and arrows of good-government critics, whereas a mass vote in the Crown's favor provides each legislator with political cover. Two equilibria are possible in pure strategies: if legislators expect that other legislators will vote with the Crown, then they will do so as well in order to obtain the small bribe on offer, but they will not do so if they expect that other legislators will vote against the Crown. The implication is that if legislators do vote with the Crown, they will sell out for an aggregate bribe less than the total benefits to the Crown of the enactment: "democratic legislators may refuse to sell a statute at all (a Nash equilibrium), or they may sell it cheap (another Nash equilibrium), but they will not sell it dear."[18] In this model, the same bribe is offered to each legislator. In a variant that allows discriminatory offers, the Crown can exclude the unfavorable equilibrium of rejection by all legislators by offering a small bribe to just a decisive majority.[19]

A second interpretation[20] drops the assumption that there is a private cost to legislators of voting with the Crown when other legislators do not, and assumes instead that all legislators dislike the Crown's policy and thus incur some private cost if the Crown's policy is enacted, regardless of what other legislators do.[21] Here the Crown has a neat trick: it may offer each voter a large amount[22] for providing the pivotal vote in the Crown's favor, a token amount for a nonpivotal vote in the Crown's favor, and nothing for a vote with the opposition.[23] Any given legislator then reasons that whether a majority of others vote either for or against, he does best by voting with the Crown, and if he is pivotal, he does best by voting with the Crown.[24] However, because all legislators reason this way, all vote with the Crown, *none* provides the pivotal vote, and the Crown obtains a decisive bloc of votes in its favor while paying each of its voters a token amount.[25]

Here legislators are in a multilateral Prisoners' Dilemma, in which all are made worse off by aiming for individual advantage. In effect, the vote-buyer in this position both creates and exploits a fallacy of composition by treating each seller as nonpivotal taken individually, despite the fact that it is logically impossible for all voters to be non-pivotal; some seller must make the decisive contribution by providing the pivotal vote necessary to make a majority. However, the trick fails if the vote-buyer cannot condition its offer to any given voter on the decisions of other voters, or if voters can secretly collude among themselves to arrange for a bare minority to vote nay. In the latter case, a pivotal vote will (apparently) be cast, the Crown will have to pay out a large sum, and the colluding voters can divide up the gains.

In either model, the Crown exploits the logic of collective action for its own advantage, which may or may not be to the advantage of society. Legislator-sellers could benefit if they could commit to sell their votes only as a group, in which case legislators could extract the full aggregate value of their votes from the Crown. But the larger the number of legislators, the more costly coordination becomes. Divide-and-conquer tactics that may not work on a small committee of decision makers may work in a larger modern legislature or a mass election. Moreover, vote-selling is corrupt behavior condemned by public norms, so the mutual transparency needed for coordination is lacking; each legislator sells his vote in the shadows and all legislators suffer by doing so. The overall result is that, as Hume wrote in a related context, "much less property in a single hand [i.e., that of the Crown] will be able to counterbalance a greater property in several; not only because it is difficult to make many persons combine in the same views and measures; but because property, when united, causes much greater dependence, than the same property, when dispersed."[26]

Although Hume's legislative example is canonical, the relevant mechanisms can generalize to other and more modern contexts, so long as the necessary conditions are satisfied. Committee chairs, interest groups, and corporate officers or directors will sometimes be able to use the same tactics to exploit problems of aggregation and collective action within committees, multimember administrative agencies, corporate boards or groups of shareholders, and other bodies. Where this occurs, actors within the system exploit system effects—particularly the logical trick of treating every voter as nonpivotal taken individually—in ways that produce counterintuitive, and perhaps pernicious, consequences for groups and institutions.

Elections and representation. Elections, which are inherently aggregative institutions, are fertile ground for system effects, and hence also for analytic mistakes about system effects. The miracle of aggregation, discussed in chapter 1, shows that aggregation *within* elections can produce surprising effects, but so can the aggregation *of* elections across multiple offices. It is treacherous in the extreme to generalize from the features of any given election to an overall analysis of a typical democratic order, in which the variety and sheer number of elections make the political system highly complex. In a withering critique of populism, Charles Beard argued that the tendency to multiply elections inflicted self-defeating cognitive overload on the voters:

> For more than a century we have been adding burdens to the ballot, until the outcome of the tendency is the paralysis of the very control which popular election is supposed to afford.... [T]he doubter is met with the firm assertion that the people may be trusted to elect any officer, local, state or national—an assertion which quite overlooks the fundamental fact that electing *all* of them together is an entirely different matter from electing *any one* of them.[27]

Beard identified a fallacy of composition inherent in populism: even if the people benefit from exerting electoral control over any given office, they may not benefit from exerting electoral control over all (or too many) offices. In the latter situation, "the multiplicity of elective offices has overburdened the voter until his control has broken down."[28]

The sheer complexity of aggregation across multiple elections and offices also fuels the perennial debate, in American politics, about whether the president or Congress is more representative of the people's will. In a presidentialist trope that has been standard at least since Andrew Jackson, the president is said to be more representative of the nation as a whole because he is elected from a national constituency. Legislators, by contrast, are elected from state or local constituencies; according to the presidentialist logic, this causes legislators to hold a parochial perspective.[29] The implicit benchmark of representation in this argument is something like the median voter in the nation as a whole.

It has been pointed out, however, that this trope rests on a fallacy of composition.[30] Taking the median-voter benchmark as given, the proper comparison is not between the president and *any individual legislator*, but between the president and *the Congress overall*. The whole legislative body may be more representative than any legislator taken individually, because the aggregation of numerous local constituencies in a majoritarian body tends to wash out extreme preferences and beliefs. Conversely, the role of the Electoral College in presidential selection means that would-be presidents cater to a relatively narrow electoral base, possibly narrower than that of the median member of Congress.[31] Put another way, presidential elections are highly bundled; a majority may support one candidate over another, because it prefers the winner's bundle of issue positions to the loser's, yet a different majority might prefer the loser's position on any particular issue. If Congress unbundles the issues and considers them one by one, it may be able to reach a series of results that more closely approximate majority preferences.

These points address only the first level of aggregation, from individual legislators to Congress, on the one hand, and from individual voters to the Electoral College, on the other. At the second level of aggregation, one must also consider the interaction between a president and a Congress who are both somewhat unrepresentative, relative to the benchmark of the median national voter. Here it is a second-level fallacy of composition to assume that the interaction between unrepresentative lawmaking institutions must produce an unrepresentative system of lawmaking. To the contrary, the interaction between two unrepresentative institutions can result in policies that are more representative, on average, than the policies that either institution in the system would produce taken separately.

In one model, where voters can only imperfectly discipline an elected executive, adding an elected legislature that is also subject to imperfect discipline can actually increase social welfare, so long as the two imperfectly representative institutions must jointly agree on decisions.[32] Roughly, the mechanism is that because joint agreement is required, the two institutions must share the gains from diverting resources to personal rather than social benefit, and this reduces the incentives of either institution to do so. In this way, the structure of interaction increases the relative gains to both institutions of implementing the voters' preferences so as to be able to stay in office, with the prospect of obtaining more benefits in the future.[33] A properly structured interaction between two imperfect representatives can do better, from the voters' standpoint, than either representative would do alone. Although I will question the premises of this model in chapter 3, as an analytic matter it cleanly identifies a fallacy of composition: it is wrong to assume that if one imperfectly representative institution is bad, more than one such institution must necessarily be even worse.

Bicameralism. In the model described above, both institutions are directly elected by the voters in the same manner. In this sense, the model could apply with equal force not to two institutions labeled "president" and "Congress," but to the two houses of a bicameral legislature elected on the same basis. In general, splitting up policy-making between two institutions with identical composition and structure can, somewhat counterintuitively, improve results compared to a unitary institution with the same total number of members and the same basis of selection. As we have seen, an ingenious argument for legislative bicameralism is that the bare existence of two different voting bodies dampens the power of agenda setters to exploit cycling majorities.[34] It has also been argued that a "congruent" bicameral assembly, in which both chambers are elected in an identical fashion, will process information more efficiently than in a unitary body.[35]

A related point arises, however, when two or more institutions that must jointly agree to accomplish action are elected under different systems. Here, the different bases of representation in the two institutions can, through interaction, produce better results than either institution could produce alone. The classic case involves the large subset of bicameral legislatures in which the two houses are selected on different bases. In a unicameral legislature using majority rule and elected under a first-past-the-post system, just over a quarter of the electorate can set policy for the whole.[36] If, however, the legislature is bicameral, the two houses must jointly agree on policies, and a different basis of representation is used in the second chamber, then a larger electoral majority is needed to control outcomes in the legislature overall.[37]

As the requisite majority grows toward one-half, bicameralism can be justified as a device that safeguards against the tyranny of the minority and, in that sense, makes the lawmaking system more representative.[38] When the requisite majority exceeds one-half of the electorate, the justification must be that bicameralism is a safeguard against the tyranny of the majority. In the latter case, bicameralism is a functionally equivalent substitute for a supermajority voting rule in a unicameral legislature.[39]

Let me now generalize the discussion to address a large question: is the federal Constitution undemocratic? Eminent political theorists and scientists have thought so, perhaps most famously Robert Dahl.[40] More recently, Sanford Levinson has charged that the Constitution is undemocratic root and branch, and should be revised in a new constitutional convention.[41]

Levinson's argument proceeds piecemeal through the institutions of the national government and attempts to show that each is undemocratic, taken one by one. The Senate is hopelessly malapportioned;[42] the Electoral College encourages presidential candidates to cater to small segments of the national electorate who live in battleground states;[43] and the Supreme Court is somewhat disciplined by electoral majorities, but imperfectly, and only with significant lag.[44] On this account, each institution is undemocratic because it fails to implement the preferences or judgments of current national majorities.[45]

One question involves the benchmark theory of democracy Levinson uses, which equates democracy with current majoritarianism. My suggestion, however, is that even accepting that premise, there is another serious issue: the neglect of system effects. Levinson's argument overlooks that the overall constitutional system may be more democratic than the sum of its parts, defining democracy according to the very benchmark he uses.

In this setting, it is a fallacy of composition to assume that because each lawmaking institution is undemocratic taken individually, the overall system that arises from their interaction must therefore be undemocratic. Conversely, it is a fallacy of division to assume that if the overall constitutional system is democratic, then each or even any of the participant institutions must be democratic, taken one by one. In either case, the inference is flawed because it misses the possibility of interaction effects. Lawmaking institutions may interact in ways that generate a kind of *emergent democracy* at the system level, even if the components are not themselves democratic in isolation. I use "emergent" strictly in the analytic sense of an emergent property—a system-level property that need not characterize all or even any of the system's component parts, here lawmaking institutions. I do not mean to connote the very different idea that legal and political institutions evolve toward democracy.

How exactly might institutional interactions, within an overall constitutional order, produce system-level democracy? The basic mechanism involves *offsetting failures of democracy*. A departure from the democratic benchmark by one institution might compensate for a departure from the democratic benchmark by another institution, in a different direction. What is important is that the failures of democracy across the array of institutions should be uncorrelated or negatively correlated, running in different and perhaps even opposite directions. A broadly egalitarian distribution of undemocratic power may produce a tolerable approximation of democracy at the systemic level, by granting many different groups a privileged forum (a different forum in each case) in which to express their views or values, or by forcing all holders of democratically objectionable legal powers and entitlements to come to the bargaining table in order to get anything done.

On this account, even if it is true that "none of the great institutions of American politics can plausibly claim to speak for the majority of Americans, even though all assert such claims,"[46] those institutions do not all depart from the majoritarian ideal in the same way, or in the same direction. The Senate favors small states;[47] the Electoral College favors groups with influence in battleground states,[48] which may or may not be small states;[49] the administrative state favors groups who can organize to influence agencies and congressional committees; the prestige and power of the Supreme Court benefit the legal elites who feed in the Court's wake. There is no one group or interest that is uniformly favored by each of these undemocratic institutions; undemocratic power is, in a sense, democratically distributed.

In general, the democratic critics have inconsistent and offsetting concerns, like the man with a terminal illness who worries about saving for retirement. Here is an example. Two main features of the American constitutional order are the status quo bias of the congressional lawmaking process and, at least after 1937, massive delegations of power to the executive. As to the first, democratic critics of the Constitution claim that the many vetogates in the quadricameral legislative process excessively frustrate the ability of current majorities to translate their wishes or judgments into law.[50] As to the second, some of the same critics claim that delegation to the executive makes policymaking undemocratic.[51] The president, they suggest, is often elected by national minorities because of the structure of the Electoral College,[52] and does not enjoy the democratic qualities of deliberation, multiple perspectives, and participation by all affected interests that Congress possesses[53]—a view that flips around the presidentialist arguments recounted above.

Yet these two departures from the democratic benchmark—excessive supermajoritarianism in the lawmaking process and excessive delegation to the executive—are to some degree uncorrelated or even negatively correlated; their effects tend to run in different and even opposing directions. Indeed, the massive increase in delegation to the executive during the Progressive Era and the New Deal was in part intended to be, and was defended as, the cure for the disease of excessive status quo bias in lawmaking.[54] The combination of legislative, executive, and judicial functions in the same hands—either the president acting through executive agencies, or the independent agencies—was in part designed to speed the government's reaction to changing economic and policy conditions and to increase its responsiveness to majoritarian sentiment.[55]

The upshot is that large-scale delegation can itself be justified, in part, as a second best compensating adjustment whose systemic effect is to unblock the vetogates of the national lawmaking process. From the standpoint of majoritarian democrats who criticize the Constitution in a piecemeal fashion, the first best would be to eliminate both excessively cumbersome lawmaking and excessive delegation to the executive. Given cumbersome lawmaking, however, delegation can push the whole system closer to the democratic critics' ideal of responsiveness to current majorities. Piecemeal democratic criticism of status quo bias and delegation misses this interaction effect and thus ranks the possible regimes incorrectly.

On a smaller scale, analogous points have been made in many other settings at the intersection of democratic theory and law. Many democrats criticize gerrymandering that results in noncompetitive electoral districts.[56] Taken one by one, such districts depart from some benchmark ideal of democracy, or so let us assume. However, at the systemic level, it is possible that multiple noncompetitive districts promote greater competition overall.[57] In the case of bipartisan gerrymanders:

> When the parties divide a state into politically homogeneous constituencies, the composition of the legislature is more reflective of the underlying partisan composition of the electorate. In contrast, a districting scheme that seeks to maximize district-level partisan competition could lead to a legislature wildly unrepresentative of the partisan preferences of the state's population.[58]

When aggregated at the level of the legislature, in other words, districts that are noncompetitive in different directions may have the overall property of "second-order diversity."[59]

Likewise, political parties have long been an object of suspicion from republican-democratic theorists who see parties as a type of pernicious political "faction." But it is a fallacy of composition to assume that if one faction is bad, multiple factions are worse. As I discuss at greater length in chapter 3, the cure for parties may be more parties; at the systemic level, pluralist competition among political parties helps to promote democratic values of participation, inclusion, and deliberation.[60] In such cases, a kind of democracy emerges from the interaction of partisan institutions that are undemocratic, taken one by one. Along similar second best lines, it has been shown that under plausible conditions, a partisan overseer of executive behavior will do a better job of monitoring the executive than will a nonpartisan overseer. Whereas the latter may have reputational incentives to pull its punches, "the distortions caused by a partisan overseer's desire to affect the executive's reputation [for the worse] can offset the distortions caused by her desire to enhance her own."[61]

EMERGENT DEMOCRACY AND CONSTITUTIONAL REFORM

These points cast doubt on the majoritarian democrats' proposals for a constitutional convention. As the general theory of second best indicates, unless *all* of the critics' prescriptions are adopted simultaneously—and surely at least some will be ruled out by politics—then even a committed majoritarian democrat might prefer the current constitutional order. If, for example, the convention reins in executive lawmaking but leaves the quadricameral lawmaking process unchanged, status quo bias will strangle current majorities. In general, because of the causal forces that operate in politics, constitutional changes must be effected through "interdependent packages."[62] If so, then simply urging as many piecemeal majoritarian changes as possible may produce far worse results, even on majoritarian grounds, than the constitutional status quo.

This caution itself has two limits. First, it does not show that bad consequences will always result from piecemeal reform; all it shows is that piecemeal reform is not always best, because approximating the good as closely as possible can sometimes produce the worst possible outcomes. It then becomes necessary to go beyond the democratic critiques by offering a detailed systemic analysis of the conditions of American constitutional democracy to see whether the interaction among particular reforms will improve matters. Second, the possible adverse consequences of piecemeal reform apply just as much to judicial updating of the Constitution through "interpretation" as to the output of constitutional conventions.[63] Whichever process is used to effect constitutional reform, an understanding of system effects and of the general theory of second best is indispensable.

THE "COUNTERMAJORITARIAN DIFFICULTY"

We have been discussing a piecemeal critique of national lawmaking institutions, stated by majoritarian democrats. An important special case is a critique of the Supreme Court's power of constitutional judicial review, also stated by majoritarian democrats. The "countermajoritarian difficulty" is the claim that the Supreme Court's power to overturn statutes on constitutional grounds is inconsistent with the constitutional order's deep commitment to majoritarian democracy.[64] The phrase itself originated with Alexander Bickel, but it has a long history and periodically reappears, in changing forms.[65]

Here there are several analytic pitfalls that only a systemic analysis can identify. It is a fallacy of division to assume that if the overall constitutional order is to be democratic, the Supreme Court must itself act democratically. Conversely, it is a fallacy of composition to assume that if the Supreme Court acts undemocratically, then the constitutional system will be undemocratic overall. An undemocratic Court may be necessary to produce a constitutional order that is democratic overall, perhaps because it is needed to offset legislative failures, where failure is defined according to the very benchmark the Court's democratic critics use.

In other words, an undemocratic Court might be indispensable to the workings of democracy, either because it polices the processes of democratic lawmaking, as in John Hart Ely's theory of judicial review;[66] because an undemocratic Court contributes to a desirable overall package of supermajoritarianism;[67] or because the Court produces errors that are negatively correlated with those of the legislative process, a possibility I will discuss below. Whether or not judicial review can indeed be justified on such grounds, as a substantive matter, is a question with empirical and prescriptive components as well as normative ones.[68] But it is an analytic mistake, rather than an empirical one, to argue from the premise that the overall constitutional order should be democratic to the conclusion that an undemocratic Supreme Court must be undesirable.

A more subtle version of the problem can be discerned in a recent and important defense of judicial review.[69] This defense begins with the striking observation that the Supreme Court's constitutional agenda[70]—the number and type of constitutional cases the Court hears—is much smaller than the nation's agenda, or the number and type of public issues that are of national concern at any given time. The Court intervenes to override democratic outcomes in only a small subset of the overall space of issues, due to constraints of politics and institutional capacity. The implication is that the countermajoritarian difficulty is overstated. On this view, "the distance between the Court's activities and the public's major concerns—the relatively small number of decisions the Court actually removes from what the public would desire to control directly—calls into question much of the contemporary and not-so-contemporary angst about the coun-termajoritarian or antidemocratic behavior of the Court."[71] Hence, "the judicial incursion on democracy—if an incursion it is—is quite a bit smaller in quantity and aggregate consequence than might be thought."[72]

However, this argument risks committing a fallacy of division. Even if constraints of politics and of institutional capacity ensure the Court cannot and does not intervene *everywhere*, it might still be the case that the Court can intervene *anywhere*. The countermajoritarian diffi-culty would then retain a valid core, stated at the level of the Court's unbounded potential to intervene rather than the actual deployment of its resources. That unbounded potential generates legal uncertainty and shapes the anticipated reactions of other institutions, creating the kind of "judicial overhang"[73] that democratic critics of the Court find debilitating. It remains true that the judicial incursion on democracy is quantitatively limited, but the "aggregate consequence[s]"[74] are amplified by uncertainty about where the incursion will take place.

Until recently, it had been argued and widely assumed that the Court would not intervene to invalidate executive action clearly autho-rized by statute that implicated military matters and foreign policy during a time of war. That idea went by the boards when the Court decided *Boumediene v. Bush*,[75] which dismissed any suggestion that de facto sovereignty over nominally foreign territory, held and used for military purposes, would pose a political question not justiciable by the courts, and which then went on to invalidate the statute authorizing executive action as a deprivation of the privilege of habeas corpus— the first such invalidation in the nation's history. The seeming lesson of *Boumediene* is that legal doctrine places few, if any, remaining con-straints on the Court's potential to intervene on any issue that a majority of the justices see as posing constitutional questions. That the Court's resources are limited ensures that universal government by judiciary is impossible; but it is universally true that government by judiciary is possible in any given area.

JUDICIAL BIAS

I turn now to the judicial system—to the structure of the courts and of judicial decision-making, focusing especially on the question of judicial "bias." Although chapter 5 focuses on the judiciary, it does so from the internal standpoint of judges. Here I examine the judiciary from the external standpoint of an analyst, or of a designer of the judicial system, such as a constitutional framer.

From an external standpoint, judicial system effects can arise at two distinct levels. First, at the level of multimember judicial panels such as the Supreme Court, the court as a whole can constitute a system whose behavior differs from the behavior of the individual judges who sit on the court. If, for example, the political biases of individual judges cut in different directions, the court as a whole can behave as though all judges are principled law-followers. Second, the interaction between the judiciary and other branches can constitute a system whose behavior differs from that of the institutions that are components of the system. Here the biases of the judiciary, on the one hand, and the legislature, on the other, can offset each other and thereby ensure that the system as a whole maximizes welfare.

The judicial miracle of aggregation. Suppose that many or most justices are "biased" in the political or partisan sense.[76] Their votes tend to track the party platforms or the policy preferences of appointing presidents. In cases of constitutional and statutory interpretation and administrative law, these justices tend, in a statistically significant fashion, to vote consistently for conservative or liberal policies as the case may be. Many studies have shown something of the kind; although long-standing, and ever-growing, this body of work has recently been dubbed "the New Legal Realism."[77]

But through a systemic lens, it is apparent that widespread judicial bias has unclear implications. First, widespread bias among the *justices* need not mean that the *court* makes biased decisions; everything depends upon how those biases are distributed. Under certain conditions, we might witness a judicial miracle of aggregation, in which highly biased justices interact in such a way that the court as a whole acts as though unbiased.

Suppose that the court has nine members, and that eight out of nine are thoroughgoing partisans who always vote their partisan preferences. One justice, however, is a sincere legalist who always votes for the correct legal answer with perfect accuracy. (This assumption is merely for simplicity; the point holds so long as the legalist justice votes with even a slight bias toward the correct answer.) Suppose also that there is always a correct legal answer, even in the hard cases that reach the court, but that the eight partisans will vote randomly from the standpoint of identifying the correct answer; partisan views are intrinsically uncorrelated with the legally correct approach and from a legal standpoint the partisans do not systematically err in any particular direction. Under majority rule, with a binary choice, the average competence of the court's members will be 0.56,[78] and the court as a whole will vote for the correct answer with an approximate probability of 0.64.[79]

This implies nothing at all about the desirability of vesting issues in the court. For one thing, the swing justice might vote sincerely but incompetently. If he votes worse than randomly—that is, with a systematic bias against the truth—then the court as a whole will display a bias toward error. Moreover, I have said nothing yet about the comparative epistemic competence of the court and other institutions, or about the court's marginal contribution to the overall epistemic system.

The point of interest is just that overwhelming and easily detected partisan bias among the justices is perfectly compatible with a bias toward legal accuracy at the level of the court as a whole.

A nightmare of aggregation. However, exactly the same logic might work in reverse, causing the court as a whole to behave in a politically biased fashion even though the vast majority of its members follow the law. Suppose that eight of the nine justices always vote according to their best understanding of the relevant law, and that this best understanding is random with respect to the liberal-conservative spectrum. Suppose also, however, that one justice is a crude political partisan who always votes his, or his party's, policy preferences. Because the eight legalist justices are random with respect to ideology, they will sometimes split their votes four to four in hard cases, where there are reasonable legal arguments cutting both ways. Then, in a kind of nightmare of aggregation, the partisan justice will occupy the swing position, thereby determining outcomes for the Court as a whole. This assumes that all the justices vote sincerely, not strategically, although one votes based on political attitudes while the others vote based on their best understanding of the relevant law. I take up the distinction between sincere and strategic judicial behavior in chapter 5. The point is just that under plausible conditions, the court will behave as a highly partisan institution even though almost all of its members are sincere legalists.

The current Court. Do we in fact see a judicial miracle of aggregation on the current Supreme Court? Or perhaps a nightmare scenario? The Court routinely splits five to four in cases of political import, with Justice Kennedy as the swing voter. And Justice Kennedy may well be the least partisan justice on the current Court. In administrative law, for example, he is equally likely to vote to invalidate conservative and liberal agency decisions.[80] Plausibly, Justice Kennedy votes sincerely, in the sense that he votes without political bias.

This does not at all exclude the possibility that the Court as a whole behaves with low aggregate competence, despite the sincerity of its swing voter. Justice Kennedy's relative lack of partisan bias does not at all guarantee that his legal theories are good ones, or that they track the truth about what the law really holds, or anything of that sort. However, it does exclude the nightmare of aggregation described above, in which the presence of a partisan swing justice causes the court as a whole to behave in a highly partisan fashion even though most of its members are sincere legalists.

Offsetting biases in the lawmaking system. So far, we have seen that a first-level system effect can arise when the votes of individual judges are aggregated into the behavior of a court. There is also a second-level system effect that can arise when courts interact with other institutions. To isolate this effect, let us assume that the Supreme Court as a whole behaves in a politically biased fashion (in some direction or other). For simplicity, we may also assume that what is true of the Court is true of the whole federal judiciary, ignoring that the Court only partially controls what the federal judiciary does. I assume here, in other words, that "the judges" as a cadre show a discernible and systematic bias in a particular direction. Currently, the federal judiciary plausibly shows an overall bias in a conservative direction; some 60 percent of current federal appellate judges were appointed by Republican presidents.[81]

As important recent work has emphasized, however, aggregate judicial bias does not at all guarantee that the lawmaking system as a whole will reach biased results, even if the judges have the last word through constitutional judicial review.[82] Indeed, the lawmaking system will not necessarily behave in biased fashion even if both Congress and the judiciary are biased, so long as their biases run in offsetting directions.[83] In the simplest version,[84] suppose that Congress enacts two types of statutes: some create public goods that make all better off, while others allocate rents to constituents of the dominant political party, and thereby reduce overall welfare. The judiciary reviews all statutes on constitutional grounds, and is able to discern which category each statute falls into. The judges, whose biases run in favor of the constituents of the legislative minority, and thus run *against* the biases of the controlling legislative majority, give deference to the statutes creating public goods but give heightened scrutiny to the rent-allocating statutes, validating the former but invalidating the latter. Under such circumstances, the overall lawmaking system will tend to weed out welfare-reducing statutes while enacting statutes that create public goods.

In this example, it is not that the judges are attempting to promote overall welfare. The judiciary is just as biased as the legislature; if the legislature had different biases, and were to enact welfare-reducing statutes allocating rents to the constituents favored by the judges, the judges would validate those statutes. The trick that makes the judges behave as though motivated to promote overall welfare, and that therefore makes the lawmaking system welfare-enhancing overall, is that the pool of statutes that the legislature enacts is itself tilted against the judiciary's biases. Lacking any ability to change the composition of the pool, the biased judiciary can do no better than to weed out, on partisan grounds, the statutes that are welfare-reducing.

This point underscores the second best logic of the argument. The first-best system would be one in which the judiciary is itself unbiased. In that case, the judiciary could simply weed out all welfare-reducing statutes while validating statutes that create public goods. Suppose, however, that the first-best is unattainable; suppose, for example, that the appointments process produces a cadre of judges who show systematic overall bias in a given direction. Even in the presence of a biased judiciary of this sort, it does not follow that the lawmaking system will be biased overall; one must compare the direction of judicial and legislative biases. It is thus a fallacy of division to assume that the lawmaking system can be unbiased only if each of its components is unbiased in its own right.[85]

System effects and the New Legal Realism. The analytic consequence of all this is that the New Legal Realism is at best incomplete, because it fails to take account of system effects. Much of the New Legal Realism is devoted to assessing the voting behavior of individual judges—including how the behavior of individual judges is affected by the behavior of other judges, through mutual conformism, the threat of whistle-blowing, and other "panel effects."[86] In light of the system effects discussed above, however, we can see that the *aggregate distribution* of votes matters as much as their content, taken individually. The New Legal Realism misses benign invisible-hand possibilities at two levels: the level of multimember courts, which may behave in legalist fashion even if most of their members vote in a highly partisan fashion most of the time, and the level of the overall lawmaking system, which may succeed in promoting overall welfare even if no actors within the system are attempting to do so, and even if the judiciary displays systematic biases that do not track overall welfare.

Even if judges are political, courts may not be. To be sure, courts might turn out to be political anyway, depending on how the votes of their members are distributed. Yet systemic analysis here identifies a major pitfall, into which a great deal of New (or old) Legal Realism stumbles. Analyzing the voting behavior of individual judges, even including panel effects, does not suffice to decide whether courts behave politically.

CONSTITUTIONAL STRUCTURE AND SYSTEMIC ANALYSIS

Whatever the merits of the foregoing claims, taken one by one, I hope that their aggregate import is clear. The subject of constitutional structure is a natural one for systemic analysis, at both levels of aggregation. As I have tried to show, the casual intuitions of legal theorists about both individual interactions within institutions, and the institutional interactions themselves, are suspect; in many cases they turn out to be fallacious. Only a rigorous systemic analysis can spot the pitfalls that threaten analysts of constitutional structure, as well as constitutional designers.

CHAPTER 3

Dilemmas of the Invisible Hand

The notion of the "invisible hand" has already surfaced at several crucial junctures. As I attempted to show in the last chapter, invisible-hand reasoning is a central organizing idea of the structural constitution, and thus underpins Madisonian constitutionalism, the separation of powers, and checks and balances. As we will see in this chapter, structurally similar reasoning occurs in many other contexts as well, including free speech, criminal and civil adjudication, and property rights. Wherever it appears, invisible-hand reasoning illustrates systemic analysis and provides provocative examples—valid or specious—of systemic reasoning. Invisible-hand arguments are intrinsically systemic: they suppose that an overall system of interaction, whether in an economic market, a constitution of separated powers, or a criminal trial, may have properties that do not characterize any of the acts or actors who interact to create that system, and that the actors within the system need not intend to bring about.

The specific aims of the chapter are twofold. The first is to identify general conditions under which an invisible-hand justification of a given legal or political institution will succeed, in the modest sense that the justification is internally coherent and plausible (whether or not true in fact). The second aim is to identify several theoretical puzzles about invisible-hand justifications that cut across the local contexts in which such justifications are offered. I believe these puzzles are, in fact, genuine and irreducible dilemmas, which arise from the systemic structure and nature of invisible-hand reasoning.

The first is the *dilemma of norms*. Norms of truth-seeking, public-regarding action, or altruism can both promote and undermine the workings of the invisible hand. Although it is abstractly possible to identify the conditions under which one effect or the other will predominate, the relevant norms are lumpy and cannot be fine-tuned sufficiently well to capture all, but only, the conditions under which norms are beneficial.

Next is the *dilemma of second best*. In a range of interesting cases, partial compliance with the conditions for an invisible-hand justification produces the worst of all possible worlds. The result is that such justifications have a knife-edged quality: either a move to full compliance *or* a move to full rejection will prove superior to the intermediate case of partial compliance. Where this is so, institutional designers face an all-or-nothing choice, with high stakes.

Finally, there is a *dilemma of verification*. In many cases, theorists claim that an invisible-hand process functions as a Hayekian discovery procedure, producing information that a centralized decision-maker could not obtain. The question whether that claim holds is empirical, but it begs the question to judge the success of the invisible-hand process by comparing it to the body of information held by any single mind (such as the analyst's) or by some centralized institution. It follows that invisible-hand justifications resting on informational benefits will necessarily have a speculative quality, but by the same token it will be intrinsically difficult to assemble decisive evidence against them.

INVISIBLE-HAND JUSTIFICATIONS

The most famous invisible-hand justification was pioneered by Adam Smith[1] and later elaborated in neoclassical economics: under conditions of perfect competition, markets will produce allocative and productive efficiency, and (hence) Pareto efficiency. In Friedrich Hayek's variant of the argument for markets, the market coordinates the decentralized information and tacit knowledge distributed throughout society, coordinating individual plans better than could any central planner.[2] Legal and political theorists have adapted these arguments to offer invisible-hand justifications for a range of institutions. Here are some of the most prominent, although the list is by no means comprehensive:

- As chapter 2 discussed, James Madison argued, under the influence of the Scottish Enlightenment, that a system of checks and balances by separated powers would protect liberty, as the unintended by-product of "ambition counteract[ing] ambition."[3]
- Following Madison, modern theorists have argued that the system of separated powers with checks and balances produces a "spontaneous order," through Coasean bargaining among lawmaking institutions.[4]
- Madison and other framers of the American Constitution were suspicious of political parties, on the traditional civic-republican ground that parties are harmful "factions." However, following Hume, Madison recognized that the cure for the evils of party might be competition among multiple parties.[5] Under pluralism

in a large federal republic, each party serves as a check upon the others;[6] the unintended by-product of their interaction is freedom from majoritarian oppression and promotion of the "general good."[7]

- Justice Oliver Wendell Holmes, Jr., adapting an idea developed by John Stuart Mill,[8] argued for free speech on the ground that "the best test of truth is the power of the thought to get itself accepted in the competition of the market."[9] Truth arises as an unintended by-product of the market for ideas.

- A close relative of Holmes's approach is Alexander Bickel's analysis of the struggle between government and journalists over the disclosure of classified government information. Bickel argued for a regime in which government may prosecute officials who leak government information, but would be barred by free-speech principles from prosecuting reporters for publishing such information (absent a narrow category of very serious harms, for example to ongoing military operations). That regime, he suggested, would result in an "unruly contest" between a government biased toward secrecy and journalists biased toward disclosure; the contest would produce an "optimal" level of disclosure overall.[10]

- The American system of criminal procedure has been compared to a market, in which legislatures set background entitlements and the "price" of crime is set by decentralized bargaining over sentences among prosecutors, defense lawyers, and judges.[11]

- James Fitzjames Stephen argued that although "the inquisitorial theory of criminal procedure is beyond all question the true one," and a trial "ought to be a public inquiry into the truth," nonetheless "it may be, and probably is, the case, that in our own time and country, the best manner of conducting such an inquiry is to consider the trial mainly as a litigation, and to allow each party to say all that can be said in support of their own view; just as the best means of arriving at the truth in respect of any controverted matter of opinion might be, to allow those who maintained opposite views to discuss the matter freely and in public."[12]

- In a generalization of Stephen's claim, one main argument for the adversary system of litigation is that decentralized production of information by competing parties will produce a closer approximation to truth than an inquisitorial system. As a corollary, some legal ethicists have argued that the adversary system excuses advocates from moral obligations that would otherwise attach,[13] although others hotly disagree.[14]

- Law-and-economics theorists have suggested that under certain conditions the common law will evolve toward efficiency, in the sense that the rules maximize aggregate wealth. In the classic models, efficiency arises because inefficient precedents impose deadweight losses and are thus more likely to be challenged.[15] A more recent variant considers conditions under which the common law evolves toward a type of informational efficiency, in the sense that all material distinctions are incorporated into the legal rules.[16] In both classes of models, efficiency arises through an invisible-hand process, as the unintended by-product of action by litigants and judges.

- The economist Harold Demsetz suggested[17] that "property rights emerge when the social benefits of establishing such rights exceed their social costs."[18] Although Demsetz's original argument took no clear position on whether this development required a "conscious endeavor,"[19] later reconstructions posit an invisible-hand process in which efficient property rights evolve as the unintended consequence of decentralized action.[20]

Put side by side, these arguments are highly heterogeneous. The most notable difference is that they point to different goods, such as liberty, welfare, and truth. But they have a common systemic structure. In every case, some good arises as an unintended by-product of decentralized action. The overall system, in other words, produces a good that none of its components can individually produce, and that none of its components may even intend to produce.

To unpack this structure, I suggest that an invisible-hand justification combines (1) an *explanation* that identifies an invisible-hand process with (2) a *value theory* that identifies some social benefit arising from the invisible-hand process and (3) a *mechanism* that explains how the invisible-hand process produces that benefit, at the aggregate level of the overall system. Although condition (3) is my central concern, I will begin with a few remarks on the first two conditions as well.

As to condition (1), I will follow Edna Ullmann-Margalit in supposing that an interesting invisible-hand explanation is one that takes as an input the preferences (or desires or goals) and beliefs of agents,[21] and that yields as an output a structured pattern of behavior.[22] The invisible-hand explanation substitutes for an explanation from design, based upon the intentional action of some designer(s).[23] A hallmark of invisible-hand explanations is that none of the participants within the system need intend to bring about the structured pattern that arises from their actions.[24] This excludes mechanisms such as the Condorcet Jury Theorem, discussed in chapter 1. When the theorem's conditions hold, the law of large numbers amplifies individual competence, but in the standard version the individuals are assumed to be attempting to figure out the right answer for the group; thus the right answer does not arise as an *unintended* by-product of their actions.

However, condition (1) does not entail that the invisible-hand system must *itself* emerge through an invisible-hand process, although it may do so. The emergence and the operation of invisible-hand systems are different questions.[25] Some explicit markets, for example, grow up through the decentralized action of many participants, whereas others arise as the result of intentional action, as when regulators design and impose a system of emissions trading. Thus top-level managers at Hewlett-Packard set up an internal prediction market in which mid-level managers would place bets on the firm's sales in future periods—bets that, when aggregated by the prediction market, in effect collected and transmitted to their superiors valuable information that was previously dispersed throughout the firm.[26] Systemic properties can emerge through deliberate engineering by intentional agents, who anticipate by-products that may be unintended or surprising to the participants in the system themselves.

Invisible-hand justifications are heterogeneous on this dimension. Some arguments, such as the claims that the common law and property rights evolve toward efficiency, are diachronic and focus on the genesis of institutions or rules. Others are synchronic and focus on the operation of institutions or rules at a given time, regardless of how those institutions or rules originated. The Madisonian argument for checks and balances attempts to justify an invisible-hand arrangement that resulted from an intentional act of constitutional design by Madison and other framers, rather than arising through an invisible-hand process. Yet the same argument could be used to justify a regime of checks and balances that evolved organically, as in legal systems that have no written constitution.

An explanation that satisfies condition (1) posits an equilibrium or spontaneous order; it thus excludes random or chaotic behavior. However, merely satisfying condition (1) need not at all imply that the spontaneous order is in any way desirable or beneficial.[27] The Tragedy of the Commons, for example, is a spontaneously arising structured equilibrium of waste and inefficiency. Accordingly, condition (2) requires the theorist to posit some systemic good that the spontaneous order produces, turning the explanation into a justification.

On this dimension as well, invisible-hand justifications are highly heterogeneous. In the neoclassical argument for markets, the relevant good is *welfare*, which markets are said to maximize. In a more recent version, the argument is that the market mechanism conduces to *freedom*, understood as the realization of individual opportunities and autonomy.[28] In the Madisonian arguments for checks and balances and for a plurality of parties, the main good is political *liberty*, although Madison also argued vaguely that freedom from factional oppression would conduce to "justice and the general good."[29] In the Holmesian argument for the marketplace of ideas, the relevant good is *truth* or, less grandly, *information*; the same goods are relevant under Stephen's argument for the adversary system of litigation.

Moreover, these goods may be combined in complex ways. The Hayekian variant of the argument for explicit markets has a hybrid character: welfare is still the ultimate good that markets produce, but instead of being produced directly by the consummation of all desired trades as in the neoclassical argument, welfare is produced indirectly by the market's ability to exploit dispersed information and even generate information that would not otherwise exist.[30] This contrast, between a directly welfarist and an informational argument for markets, is analogous to the contrasting arguments for the efficiency of the common law: the standard argument focuses exclusively on wealth-maximization through the weeding out of inefficient rules, while the more recent hybrid argument suggests that the common law evolves toward informational efficiency.

Given all this heterogeneity, it is reasonable to question whether there is even a coherent category of invisible-hand justifications in the first place. I believe that the common structure of these arguments, in which systemic goods are produced as the unintended by-product of decentralized action, gives rise to important common problems, but the proof of this must emerge from the subsequent discussion. The points I will make below are addressed to the common structure of the arguments and thus do not depend upon whether the argument has a diachronic or synchronic character, and—with one exception—do not depend upon the nature of the relevant good. The exception is that the dilemma of verification—the justification of competition as a discovery procedure creates empirical questions which by definition cannot be tested, at least in interesting cases—applies by its terms only where truth or information is the relevant good.

Condition (3), on which I will focus, requires the analyst to supply a systemic mechanism that aligns the structured pattern or spontaneous order of condition (1) with the social benefit identified to satisfy condition (2). For concreteness, and to set a benchmark case, consider the economic argument for free markets in ordinary goods. In the standard welfare-economic interpretation of Smith's cursory references to the "invisible hand,"[31] the operation of the price system in perfectly competitive markets will produce long-run allocative and productive efficiency in which net social benefits are maximized. By definition, the conditions of allocative and productive efficiency also entail Pareto efficiency. In this argument, the price system is the relevant mechanism (condition 3) that ensures that the behavior of actors under perfect competition produces a system-level equilibrium (condition 1) that maximizes social welfare (condition 2).

In a number of invisible-hand justifications, this crucial third condition either is not clearly satisfied or else is clearly not satisfied. As an example of the former problem, the argument that decentralized bargaining in the American system of criminal procedure creates a "market price" for crime[32] does not clearly posit any mechanism that aligns individual behavior with the relevant systemic good, here social welfare. The sentences themselves, whether set in terms of jail time or in monetary fines, are numerical, continuously graded, and plausibly commensurable, so that the analogy to the price system can at least be offered with a straight face. However, it is hardly clear that this suffices to align private and social costs. Genuinely irrational actors, insensitive to price changes, might be selected out of markets through bankruptcy but selected *into* the criminal system by their inability to respond to the law's deterrent signals. Although changes in the "price" of crime through increased sentences will affect rational criminals and thus change behavior at the margin,[33] if the fraction of rational criminals is very small, those changes will also be marginal in the colloquial sense. Furthermore, punishment through incarceration, as opposed to fines, builds in a systematic misalignment between private and social costs, because the punishment itself requires social expenditures for the infrastructure of punishment—prisons and guards.[34] That extra social cost cannot be entirely folded into the private cost of crime by increasing the expected sentence, because the social cost would then increase as well—unless the costs of running the prison system are all fixed rather than marginal costs, which is implausible.

More generally, the system of criminal procedure might better be described not as a genuine market but as a system of sequential decision-making by autonomous monopolies, in which the prosecutor has near-unchecked discretion over whether to charge a crime, the jury has near-unchecked discretion over whether to acquit, and the judicial system has near-unchecked discretion over final review of convictions. Although the prosecutor bargains with the defendant's lawyer over the conditions of the plea, the relevant "prices" are set by the parties' anticipation of what the judge and jury might eventually do, and there is no bargaining between the prosecutor and the jury, the prosecutor and the judges, or the jury and the judges. In competitive markets, by contrast, the price at which A will buy from B is defined by the next-best terms A and B could agree to with another buyer and seller, not by the terms some third party would impose upon them. Moreover, even if there were simultaneous bargaining among prosecutor, jury, judge, and defendant, the theory of bargaining under multilateral monopoly is notoriously indeterminate, so it would be hard to say whether a system of this sort conduces to efficiency however defined. The market analogy here is thus noticeably attenuated.

An example of clear failure to satisfy the third condition is Demsetz's original argument for the evolution of efficient property rights, which posited conditions under which such rights would be socially efficient, but offered no mechanism to explain why the relevant groups would move toward the efficient regime. Later analysts have attempted to supply such a mechanism by positing various invisible-hand processes conducing to efficiency, yet there are equally plausible interest-group accounts suggesting that property rights need not be efficient at all.[35] The latter accounts parallel a standard argument that the common law need not evolve to efficiency. Repeat players, such as organized interest groups, have superior access to courts or differential stakes in judicial precedent and will bias the selection of cases for litigation, thereby skewing the precedents that result.[36]

More controversially, as I briefly argued in chapter 2, I believe that Madison's invisible-hand argument for a system of separated powers with checks and balances clearly fails to satisfy the third condition. Although stemming from Adam Smith,[37] Madison's argument is dissimilar in a critical respect: it does not specify any mechanism that aligns the "private" costs and benefits to institutions with social costs and benefits.[38] The decentralized bargaining among institutions that characterizes a system of separated powers with checks and balances contains nothing remotely resembling a well-defined system of explicit or implicit prices, not even in the broad sense in which criminal sentences are prices. There is no systematic reason to think that this sort of bargaining will produce efficient outcomes, somehow defined, or other benefits such as the protection of liberty.

To explain this point more fully, I will contrast bargaining in explicit economic markets with bargaining under a system of separated powers with checks and balances. The Coase theorem holds that where transaction costs are zero, actors will bargain to efficient outcomes whatever the initial allocation of entitlements. In the limiting case, the Coase theorem implies that any institutional structure is irrelevant, because actors will simply bargain around it. By contrast, a system of mutual checking by separated powers presupposes that standing institutional forms matter, and cannot be costlessly dissolved and reformed on an ad hoc basis. For this reason, models of the separation of powers in which mutual checks produce welfare benefits must assume constraints on bargaining or collusion by institutions.[39] The consequence, however, is that a system of separated powers creates externalities that cannot always be internalized through bargaining; separated institutions may inflict externalities upon one another that represent real social losses, not merely transfers. Thus another plausible model of the separation of powers shows that (1) absent bargaining, the separation of powers produces externalities between institutions and (thus) harms welfare; and (2) even with bargaining, the separation of powers can never do better than simple unitary government.[40]

Whatever the relative merits of these competing models, the transaction costs of bargaining within a system of separated powers are in any event much greater than zero; they include all manner of posturing, bluffing, brinkmanship, and holdouts. What are the properties of such a system? The legislature, president, and judiciary do bargain repeatedly over similar issues, and this produces something that vaguely resembles a marketplace for policies. Yet there are two major stumbling blocks to believing this marketplace to be efficient, in any sense. First, the institutions are themselves aggregates of individual officials with competing agendas, a great deal of agency slack between their own interests and that of the institution as such, and, especially in Congress, severe costs of coordination and collective action.[41] It thus requires an elaborate analysis of particular cases to decide whether bargains among the institutions efficiently serve even the interests of their members, let alone the interests of the ultimate principals—the citizens or voters.

Second, even if institutions were internally unified, severe commitment problems cripple the marketplace for policies. There is no institution external to government that can enforce agreements reached through institutional bargaining;[42] this absence of enforceable contracting remits the parties to self-help and tit-for-tat reputational or repeat-play mechanisms in which cooperation is merely one equilibrium. These two problems reinforce one another, because the turnover of personnel within institutions undermines the reputational mechanisms that can sometimes produce long-term cooperation even where agreements are unenforceable. Under these conditions there is no reason to think that institutional bargaining over policies systematically produces efficient results, and there can be no political Coase theorem.[43]

All this suggests that there is no general welfarist argument for the separation of powers or checks and balances. As we have seen, however, the relevant good may be political liberty, not welfare. Perhaps Madison's argument should be understood to claim that the separation of powers will protect liberty in some rough-and-ready way, by raising the costs of enacting new legislation. On this argument, the transaction costs of the system are a virtue, not a vice.

The separation of powers at the *national* level, however, only makes it difficult to enact federal legislation, remitting individuals to whatever rights they may or may not enjoy under other sources of law, including potentially oppressive state and local laws; the federal government's internal separation of powers protects federalism,[44] not liberty per se. When the multiple veto-points of the federal lawmaking process block legislation that would shield individual liberty from state and local infringements, liberty interests are harmed, not protected. Even in a unitary rather than federal lawmaking system, private action might itself impair liberty suitably defined, and the veto-points of a complex lawmaking system would then block lawmaking that would protect liberty from private infringements. At best, then, the system of separation of powers with checks and balances produces a liberty-liberty trade-off, and there is no general mechanism ensuring that the trade-off will be struck so as to maximize liberty overall. The upshot is that bargaining within a system of separated powers, even if it produces short-run mutual advantage for the institutions involved, will have no systematic tendency either to protect liberty or to produce efficient outcomes for society generally.[45]

A separate and equally serious problem is that Madison's argument does not clearly specify a mechanism by which the separation of powers, or checks and balances, generate spontaneous *order* in the first place. Not only is the system not necessarily socially beneficial, in terms of either welfare or liberty, as I have just argued; it may not even produce a patterned outcome at all. If this is so, the system's outcomes will represent a random walk depending upon a succession of political contingencies and the accidents of history, as chapter 2 suggested. The argument may thus fail condition (1) as well as condition (3).

So far I have suggested three necessary conditions for invisible-hand justifications and offered examples of arguments that fail one or more of the conditions. Even if all three conditions are met, however, all that results is a *cogent* invisible-hand justification (borrowing the term that Ullmann-Margalit applies to invisible-hand explanations).[46] The cogent explanation might or might not be true, and might or might not be justified in the sense that it is warranted by a rational assessment of the evidence. However, a major complication in assessing the truth or evidentiary warrant for invisible-hand justifications is that their proponents often argue that they are useful precisely because they disclose information that cannot be obtained in any other fashion. I shall return to that issue below.

Moreover, even if an invisible-hand justification is both cogent and true or at least justified, it need not be dispositive. There is always a further comparative institutional question: even given that an invisible-hand process can be shown to produce some social benefit, would an alternative institutional arrangement produce the same benefit at lower cost, produce more of the benefit at the same cost, or produce greater net benefits at higher cost? These questions become relevant in cases where institutional designers face the choice whether to set up invisible-hand processes to achieve their ends, or instead to use other approaches. Although Hewlett-Packard's internal prediction market worked well,[47] it is possible that alternative arrangements lacking the invisible-hand character of the prediction market would have worked equally well or even better; consider a survey of midlevel managers about whether they expect to meet production and sales targets, combined with a credible promise that the survey would be conducted on an anonymous basis, perhaps by an independent firm. In such cases, the choice between an invisible-hand arrangement and some other arrangement is a matter for ordinary cost-benefit analysis.

It is obviously somewhat arbitrary to separate out the three conditions specified above, for the cogency of invisible-hand justifications, from the further questions whether such justifications are true and dispositive. Although nothing of substance turns on this, I believe that the cogency conditions demarcate conditions under which an invisible-hand justification is in some sense entitled to compete in the marketplace of ideas with other institutional arrangements, justified by other types of arguments. If the invisible-hand justification fails because the evidence does not support it, or because there are superior alternatives, these are venial sins, whereas a failure to satisfy the cogency conditions means that the invisible-hand justification is in some sense incoherent and thus spurious, perhaps ideological.

THE DILEMMA OF NORMS

I turn now to the dilemmas that bedevil invisible-hand justifications, and that cut across the local debates in which such justifications are offered. To be clear, I do not suggest that *each* of these dilemmas applies to *every* invisible-hand justification, nor that these dilemmas apply *only* to invisible-hand justifications, as some of them apply in other contexts as well. I do suggest that (1) each of these dilemmas applies to more than one invisible-hand justification, and thus transcends particular questions or debates within legal and political theory; (2) every invisible-hand justification (of which I am aware) runs into one or more of these dilemmas, and for systematic reasons.

I begin with a set of problems arising from the role of norms in invisible-hand arguments. "Norms" are notoriously hard to define, but a rough cut suffices for my purposes: by norms, I will mean rules of conduct that oblige agents to act in a way inconsistent with their short-run interests. As we will see, one of the issues about norms is whether and when they actually serve the agents' long-run interests. I also mean to be agnostic on the question whether norms are (ever) genuinely internalized, or are observed only because agents anticipate that violations of the norms will cause others to sanction them.[48]

Norms can be social, moral, legal, or political; professional norms, such as rules of conduct for lawyers and doctors, have a hybrid character, composed of social, moral, legal, and political elements simultaneously. An important twist is that professional norms will sometimes require the professional to give effect to the self-interest of the client, as when lawyers argue that their professional role requires zealous advocacy of the client's interests. In cases of this sort, the contrast between norm-governed behavior and self-interested behavior can be recast as a tension between generally applicable norms of ethics or altruism, on the one hand, and the professional norms of specialized agents such as lawyers, on the other. The points I will offer are the same under either description of the problem.

Do norms promote or frustrate the working of the invisible hand? Both answers have champions. Academic moralists typically, and economists occasionally, suggest that moral norms of good faith and fair dealing are indispensable to the operation of markets: "good consequences in equilibrium will depend on at least some voluntary compliance with nonlegal prescriptions."[49] In the standard rendition of this claim, norms are indispensable to producing social benefits in situations of market failure. In explicit economic markets, for example, the costs of contracting and enforcing contracts make it impossible to exclude all forms of literalism, circumvention of promises, and chicanery; norms of good faith are thus necessary to facilitate exchange.[50] Likewise, in a "market for lemons"[51] characterized by asymmetric information and experience goods or credence goods, norms of truthfulness or honesty are necessary to prevent exploitation and unraveling. In the market for commercial blood donations, as of 1972, the "detection [of hepatitis in the donated blood] depend[ed] essentially on the willingness of the donor to state correctly whether or not he is suffering from that disease."[52]

Similar arguments have been applied to invisible-hand justifications for legal and political institutions. On one account of pluralist competition among political parties, partisanship is positively beneficial, but only so long as it occurs within a framework of "regulated rivalry" in which "[p]arty conflict entails political self-discipline—institutionalized, eventually legalized, internalized and made moral habit."[53] This "ethic of partisanship"[54] is necessary to keep partisan competition within bounds. Similarly, it has been argued that the market for ideas functions well only because, and to the extent that, participants observe norms of truth-seeking. On this view, truth does not arise as an unintended by-product of self-interested behavior:

> [H]istorians, for example, might arrive at a better and deeper under-standing of historical events through an open and unfettered discussion of historical evidence and alternative hypotheses. But the process works because the participants are committed to some conception of the truth and observe various standards in their presentation and assessment of evidence and theories.[55]

Finally, a standard critique of the adversary system of litigation holds that the trial cannot serve as a truth-finding device if lawyers aim solely for victory, and do not observe any norms of respect for truth.[56]

The contrary view, according to which norms hamper markets, tends to be held by economists and political scientists rather than professional moralists, and can take either of two forms. In the first version, the concern is that partial compliance with norms can be worse than either full compliance or no compliance at all. This is the dilemma of the second best, which I will take up shortly. In a second and stronger version, the concern is that even when (or especially when) they are universally observed, *norms create friction* rather than lubrication, and thus represent a drag on the processes of competition that generate a socially beneficial equilibrium in markets or other institutions. As to explicit markets, an example is the "feudal shackles thesis," which holds that the persistence of traditional norm-governed behavior into the bourgeois era hampers the full attainment of the social benefits of capitalism.[57]

Norms can create friction in several ways. For one thing, norms may not only dampen self-interested motivation, but also produce ill-informed action. "[E]thically motivated behavior may even have a negative value to others if the agent acts without sufficient knowledge of the situation."[58] Ethical motivation may be a real but relatively weak phenomenon, and thus provide a weaker spur for the acquisition of information than does rank self-interest.

For another thing, there is severe tension between *norms of reciprocity*, on the one hand, and *norms of altruism*, on the other. Reciprocity can support the generation of efficient conventions or the production of public goods by inducing sanctions against violators or free riders, but altruism can undermine those incentives by causing putative sanctioners to empathize with the pain of those who stand to be sanctioned.[59] To be sure, in some cases, altruism might instead *support* sanctioning of norm violators or free riders. Under "altruistic punishment," individuals are willing to incur personal costs to punish violation of social norms, even without repeated play. In single-shot dictator games, in which player A can allocate a fixed surplus between herself and player B, it has been found that a third party C who has no stake in the allocation may incur a personal cost to punish A-players who allocate more than half the surplus to themselves.[60] The problem, then, can be understood as the *indeterminacy of altruism*: in many contexts, the altruist has to choose between empathy with the party who stands to be sanctioned, and empathy with those harmed by that party.

In various invisible-hand settings, legal theorists suggest that norms can produce harmful friction. A leading criticism of Bickel's contest theory, under which a struggle between government and press over disclosure of secret information will produce a socially beneficial equilibrium, holds that the adversarial model on which the [contest] theory relies is both odd and inaccurate. It requires an assumption that the government and private speakers are locked in combat, with each trying constantly to undermine the other. It would be disturbing if such a picture mirrored reality. *The normal expectations are that the press will at least sometimes respect legitimate interests in secrecy, and that the government will often promote disclosure on its own.* If the incentives diverge dramatically from what the equilibrium model assumes, the model will break down.[61]

This passage suggests that norms of mutual restraint, observed by both government and press, are precisely what prevent the contest from working at full power. This illustrates a larger issue: if norms are friction, rather than lubricant, then invisible-hand justifications imply that *norms are obstructions to be removed.* The critic quoted above is implicitly attempting to discredit the contest theory by showing that fully implementing the logic of that theory would require a "disturbing" violation of norms of political morality. Yet the opposite conclusion might also be drawn: if the contest theory is otherwise correct, so that relevant norms block the attainment of a social optimum, the norms rather than the theory should give way.

So far I have tried to lay out two conceptions of the relationship between norms and the operation of the invisible hand, involving norms as lubrication and as friction respectively. Can these conceptions be reconciled? Perhaps each is correct, just under different circumstances. On this view, where there are serious background imperfections in the relevant market, norms are necessary lubricants, but where markets otherwise operate smoothly, norms hamper the attainment of the welfare-maximizing equilibrium that would arise through universally self-interested action. Kenneth Arrow thus states, "I think it best on the whole that the requirement of ethical behavior be confined to those circumstances where the price system breaks down [because of asymmetric information and other market failures]."[62] Norms should be turned off where markets function well, and turned on where they do not.[63]

While this reconciliation is attractive in theory, it overlooks that *norms cannot be perfectly fine-tuned*; they cannot be tailored to any arbitrarily desired degree of nuance and suspended or activated at will. First, it is implausible that the same actors who behave in a fully self-interested fashion in the absence of market failure will be able to fully adhere to a constraining code of norms in the presence of market failure. Either self-interested behavior will spill over from the domain where it is socially beneficial into the domain where it is not, or the norm-based constraints that are desirable in the latter domain will also shape behavior in the former, where they are undesirable. Smith famously quipped that "[p]eople of the same trade seldom meet together, even for merriment and diversion, but the conversation ends in a conspiracy against the public, or in some contrivance to raise prices."[64] Economic agents who ruthlessly seek profits in competitive markets will also tend to collude in order to make markets noncompetitive. The standard remedy is to police those agents through antitrust and competition law, but this requires a separate and costly apparatus of legal rules and institutions, extrinsic to Arrow's norm-based framework.

Second, the processes of reputational sanctioning and moral education, by which institutions and individuals force others to observe or even to internalize norms, depend for their effectiveness, in part, on the dogmatic and general character of the norms themselves. While some norms take the form of a presumption that can be overcome, or a rule-with-exceptions, the principle that actors should act on the basis of general norms only under conditions of "market imperfection" has a different structure, in which the norm is rendered wholly operative or inoperative by vague background conditions. Not only is it psychologically costly to switch norms on and off in this fashion, but the switching condition is itself ill-defined.

Finally, there is a problem about how the requisite norms can be generated. In the usual case, norms are not chosen by anyone in particular, and instead emerge systemically, as the unintended by-product of decentralized interactions between and among individuals and institutions. Arrow uses a passive verb ("it [is] best... that the requirement of ethical behavior be confined")[65] because it is mysterious who in society has the ability to confine norms of ethical behavior to all and only those circumstances identified by the economic theory of market failures.[66] The supply side of norms is their Achilles' heel.[67] Although there are occasional attempts to put forth an explicitly evolutionary theory to the effect that norms develop so as to patch up failures of markets, there is no general mechanism sufficiently robust to support such a theory. Inefficient conventions can harden into inefficient norms,[68] and even where norms would be efficient, their existence will depend upon the private costs and benefits to individuals of supporting those norms by sanctioning violators or by praising and conferring benefits upon entrepreneurs who pioneer efficient norms. The private calculus of norm-generation and norm-enforcement may well diverge from the social calculus of norms' efficiency.[69] Norms are most plausibly efficient within small groups whose members interact repeatedly, and who collectively bear both the costs and benefits of the norms they create, so that the group's internal norms do not impose significant externalities.[70] Yet such groups are the exception rather than the rule in large-scale and impersonal modern economies.

The proposed reconciliation, then, appears highly contingent and imperfect; there is no general reason to think it is generally feasible. If this is right, the sheer lumpiness of norms is, as it were, a kind of imperfection in the available technology for coping with market imperfections, including imperfections in the implicit markets addressed in legal theory. Where norms are lumpy, they are condemned either to overshoot the mark or to undershoot it: either norms will be absent in some cases of genuine market imperfections, or will be present in cases where they hamper the operation of markets. In this respect, the role of norms poses, I believe, a genuine and unavoidable dilemma for invisible-hand justifications.

THE DILEMMA OF SECOND BEST

We have just seen some problems that arise within explicit or implicit markets because of the operation of widely shared norms. Yet even if norms would be beneficial when widely shared, *partial* compliance with norms might make things worse, not better. This problem is a special case of the general theory of second best, introduced in chapter 1. Both as to norms and more generally, a state of affairs in which only some of the relevant variables take on their optimal values may well be inferior to a state in which no variables do so. An implication is that piecemeal "improvements," in the sense that one or a few variables are nudged toward their optimal values while others remain suboptimal, may make things worse.[71]

Chapter 1 also explained the logical connections between the general theory of second best and systemic analysis. Unsurprisingly, the general theory of second best also connects to invisible-hand justifications in a systematic way, because the theory implies that the interaction among several nonideal elements can produce an overall system that is as close as possible to the ideal. Invisible-hand justifications, which describe how some systemic good arises from the interaction of agents whose behavior is nonideal taken one by one, just apply this insight in particular settings. By the same logic, however, the general theory of second best also implies that partial compliance with the conditions for an invisible-hand justification can be the worst of all possible worlds.

Partial compliance can take the form either of *asymmetric compliance* by some and not others, or else a *moderate level of compliance* by all.[72] In the former case, asymmetric compliance with or internalization of norms by some parties and not others can cripple processes of bargaining or exchange:

> Once upon a time two boys found a cake. One of them said, "Splendid! I will eat the cake." The other one said, "No, that is not fair! We found the cake together, and we should share and share alike, half for you and half for me." The first boy said, "No, I should have the whole cake!" Along came an adult who said, "Gentlemen, you shouldn't fight about this: you should compromise. Give him three quarters of the cake."
>
> What creates the difficulty here is that the first boy's preferences are allowed to count twice in the social choice mechanism suggested by the adult: once in his expression of them and then again in the other boy's internalized ethic of sharing. And one can argue that the outcome is socially inferior to that which would have emerged had they both stuck to their selfish preferences.[73]

As for the latter case, it has been argued, as to explicit markets, that although an economy in which all agents are fully altruistic could function even better than an economy in which all agents are fully self-interested, under plausible conditions the worst state of affairs would be an economy in which agents are somewhat altruistic.[74] In the production of public goods, for example, fully altruistic agents might take into account that failure to sanction noncontributors will hurt all concerned, but partly altruistic agents might focus solely on the suffering that sanctioning the noncontributor will produce, resulting in inadequate sanctions and hence inadequate contributions. These arguments illustrate that while universal compliance with norms that override self-interested behavior may be best of all, partial compliance—either in the sense of compliance by some and not others, or in the sense of a moderate level of compliance by all—can be socially inferior to universal norm-free self-interest.

Structurally analogous problems of partial compliance arise in many invisible-hand settings in legal and political theory. Suppose that a system of pluralist competition among political parties requires an internalized "ethic of partisanship," according to which partisans accept an institutionalization of conflict that will result in the parties' rotation in office.[75] Suppose also, however, that not all parties internalize this ethic: most parties are restrained by norms of democratic behavior, while a few parties seek election only as a stepping-stone to permanent domination, intending to exploit democracy in order to abolish democracy. The result may be that "the best lack all conviction, while the worst are full of passionate intensity,"[76] giving an enduring advantage to the parties who unilaterally reject democratic norms (although on tactical grounds they may pretend to accept them for the time being). This is a familiar dilemma or paradox of democracy; most democracies address it by placing legal limitations on individual freedom to associate with parties who aim to subvert democracy itself.[77]

However, less worrisome configurations are also possible. If there is a group of self-restrained parties who respect the basic framework of democracy, and another group of parties who do not, the framework may nonetheless be stable if the latter group is internally divided between parties of the extreme left and extreme right. In that case, the extremes may simply thwart each other's efforts. Alternatively, although each of the extreme parties may hope for total victory, the second preference of each may be to support the democratic framework, rather than risk total victory for parties at the other extreme.

These possibilities emphasize that everything depends on the precise distribution of noncompliance across parties. The general theory of second best does not imply that partial compliance will always produce the worst of all possible worlds, only that it can do so.

Analogous problems arise in the setting of free speech. Suppose that the marketplace of ideas would function best if media institutions observe norms of truth-seeking and responsible balancing of all affected interests. Yet if only some media institutions adhere to these norms, the resulting state of affairs might be worse than if no media observed the norms at all. Political partisans are often heard to complain that media institutions are composed of (1) neutral gatekeepers and (2) propagandists of the opposite party; this creates a skew in (what the partisans take to be) the wrong direction. When they are logically consistent, these partisans go on to argue that the neutral gatekeepers should be replaced by partisans of their own view, producing a "fair and balanced" array of viewpoints at the level of the overall system rather than within individual media firms.

In this sort of case, partial compliance with the norms of objective journalism is not a sufficient condition for a distortion to arise. One possible configuration, parallel to the happy scenario in which extremist parties of left and right cancel each other out, is that some media institutions are objective, while others are partisan, yet in opposite directions; objective journalism may then rise above the fog of partisan conflict, in a miracle of aggregation for free speech. Here again, partial compliance does not entail the worst of all possible worlds, but it does make the worst-case scenario possible.

Chapter 2 argued that in the setting of checks and balances and the separation of powers, analogous problems arise when some institutions, but only some, pursue Madisonian "ambition," while others attempt to promote the public good (somehow defined).[78] Theorists of separation of powers frequently argue that a system of universal institutional ambition is inferior to a system in which all institutions observe norms of mutual self-restraint. On this view, the separation of powers "works only if every branch is committed to effective governance and is willing to forbear from the deployment of its powers to their extreme theoretical limits."[79] However, the theorists usually do not consider the consequences of partial self-restraint, by some institutions and not others. Where this occurs, *universal* institutional ambition may be the best of the attainable regimes, even if universal self-restraint would be best of all.

A final example involves the role of the prosecutor in an adversarial system of criminal procedure. In the standard view, the criminal defense lawyer's obligation is to act as a zealous advocate for the accused, a role frequently justified by the equilibrium theory that vigorous competition between self-interested parties will produce more information overall. At the same time, however, the standard view holds that the prosecutor's duty is to "seek[ ] truth and not victims"[80]— to act in the interests of public justice rather than as a partisan advocate for conviction.

These two ideas are patently in some tension with one another. One cannot simply say that the prosecutor and the defense lawyer have different roles, because the invisible-hand justification for adversarial litigation involves the systemic relationship between the two. If the premise is that the defense lawyer may be a zealous advocate because a *system* of competitive production of evidence by parties best promotes truth overall, it is not obvious how one can go on to deny that the other party, namely the prosecutor, should be equally entitled to produce evidence in a competitive and partisan fashion. A system in which prosecutors but not defense lawyers have an obligation to present evidence impartially to the tribunal might be the worst of all possible worlds. One can affirm, by brute force, that an asymmetric role-morality is most likely to produce truth overall, but that position must necessarily rest on a different theory than the invisible-hand justification for competitive production of evidence.

There are three logically consistent approaches to resolving this tension. First, one might redefine the defense lawyer's role to require disinterested truth-seeking; second, one might redefine the prosecutor's role as that of a zealous advocate for conviction; third, one might admit that the combination of zealous defense with impartial prosecution compromises the invisible-hand logic of the adversary system, but go on to argue that the compromise is justified as a means of introducing a bias in favor of the accused, which is desirable on extrinsic grounds. The first solution has its advocates.[81] As for the second, although I have not found this view endorsed as such by any legal commentator, a near relative is the view that the prosecutor's office in effect combines two functions—advocacy and impartial judgment—that should be separated, institutionally, by having different executive personnel perform the two functions.[82] The implication is that when litigating, as opposed to performing other functions, the prosecutor should be a zealous advocate for conviction.

The third solution probably captures the implicit assumptions of many criminal law theorists. On this view, a hybrid adversary system for criminal cases, one in which the prosecutor but not the defense has a duty of impartiality, is all of a piece with the requirement of a unanimous jury vote to convict, the rule that guilt must be proven beyond a reasonable doubt, and other built-in protections for the accused. This skew might in turn be justified by pointing to a background imbalance of resources between the state and the accused, by a belief that the costs of erroneous conviction are much greater than the costs of erroneous acquittal, or both.

A view of this sort would need much more work, however. Here are two of the more obvious problems:

(1) Some theory is needed to determine *how much* skew in favor of the defendant is socially desirable. Even if one believes that it is better for ten guilty defendants to go free than for one innocent defendant to be convicted, it is unlikely to be better that a thousand guilty defendants should go free.[83] If the background institutions of the jury system and of proof beyond a reasonable doubt already build in the right amount of skew, then an additional requirement that the prosecutor litigate with one hand tied beyond her back in effect double-counts the defendant's interests.

(2) Even if the background institutions do not create enough bias in the defendant's favor, it is not obvious why compromising the adversary system of litigation—stipulating that such a system is otherwise desirable on truth-production grounds—is the right means for introducing additional protections. Given some desirable amount of pro-defendant bias, the institutional designer should intervene on the margin that will produce the desired bias at the lowest social cost. Expanding juries from twelve to fifteen, for example, with a unanimous vote still required to convict, might be less costly than weakening the invisible hand of the adversary system.[84]

These examples underscore a central dilemma of invisible-hand justifications. Where partial compliance would produce the worst possible state of affairs at the systemic level, such justifications are balanced on a razor's edge: whether full compliance with the invisible-hand conditions or full rejection of those conditions is best of all, a move toward *either* extreme will represent an improvement. Moreover, starting from the state of either full or no compliance, a move by small steps toward the other extreme can be blocked by the high costs of transition through the worst-case scenario of partial compliance. The horns of the dilemma have their sharpest edge when it is uncertain whether the first-best state is or is not attainable, and when the costs of trying to reach it, but failing to do so, are high.

To make these problems concrete, suppose that in a system of separated powers the first best is a system in which all branches of government behave with a measure of self-restraint, yet none are currently doing so. Should any one branch opt for restraint, hoping that others will follow its lead? Even if all branches have Assurance Game preferences, and would thus prefer to cooperate if others do so (reciprocal cooperation), each may believe that the others have Prisoners' Dilemma preferences, and would thus prefer to defect whether or not others cooperate, in which case the cooperators will receive only the "sucker's payoff."[85] Believing this, no branch will show restraint, the beliefs of all branches about the other branches will be confirmed in a self-fulfilling fashion,[86] and the system will remain indefinitely in a second-best state. Alternatively, one branch might decide to show restraint regardless of what others do; as argued in chapter 2, under identifiable conditions this unilateral forbearance will produce the worst possible results.

THE DILEMMA OF VERIFICATION

Do invisible-hand justifications actually work, in a given domain? Across all domains, theorists recognize that the question is at least partly empirical. The preferred mode of argument is then implicitly to shift the burden of proof to the other side. One criticism of Bickel's contest theory of free speech, for example, is that "[t]he equilibrium theory remains impressionistic and relies on premises that are both unsupported and unlikely."[87] As for the broader claim that the marketplace of ideas produces truth, its "most prominent weakness" is "[t]he absence of…a demonstration, in the face of numerous counter-examples," that truth tends to prevail over falsehood.[88] Likewise, a standard criticism of the argument that the adversary system produces truth is that it is merely "a hopeful supposition derived from advocacy ideology. There is no empirical evidence indicating that the contests of advocates deliver truth in this manner."[89] Such arguments rarely explain why the invisible-hand justification should be rejected if there is no evidence for it; the situation is equally compatible with there being no evidence against it, and the lack of evidence favoring the invisible-hand justification is not the same as positive evidence that the justification fails. Absence of evidence is not the same as evidence of absence.

This implicit burden-shifting is the usual stuff of legal argument, but I believe that the empirical problems surrounding invisible-hand justifications go deeper than in many other domains. The key problem is that invisible-hand justifications often include an express or implied claim that *competition serves as a discovery procedure.*[90] The action of participants in express or implied markets itself generates information, to which the analyst may have no other means of access.

Hayek famously made this claim as to explicit economic markets, yet Hayek also suggested an analogy between markets and many other social and political institutions that harness competition, such as "sporting events, examinations, the awarding of government contracts, [and] the bestowal of prizes for poems, not to mention science." Such institutions, Hayek suggested, are justified when and because we do not otherwise know the information that the competition is designed to reveal. "It would be patently absurd to sponsor a contest if we knew in advance who the winner would be.... The only reason we use competition at all has as its necessary consequence the fact that the validity of the theory of competition can never be empirically verified *for those cases in which it is of interest.*"[91]

On the logic of this claim, we might have no independent access to the information by which to judge whether an invisible-hand justification does or does not work. As to explicit markets, the analyst who asks the question is a single mind, and on Hayekian premises can never generate the information that socially distributed knowledge can produce through the price system or analogous mechanisms. In the context of adversary criminal trials, "We can't learn directly whether the facts are really as the trier determined them because we don't ever find out the facts."[92] This is slightly overstated, because in a tiny fraction of cases DNA evidence or other conclusive proof emerges after the fact, yet it seems a valid generalization. In the setting of free speech, it might be argued—although to my knowledge no one has done so— that it is pointless to ask whether the marketplace of ideas really tends as a general matter to produce truths that cannot otherwise be discovered. Putting aside the possibility of divine revelation, it is not obvious what independent source of truth could be appealed to without begging the question.

The lack of independent access to the information supposed to be generated by competitive processes insulates Hayekian invisible-hand justifications from criticism, but the price is high. Where competition is said to function as a discovery procedure, the success of the invisible-hand justification will be *empirical but unverifiable*. This makes it just as hard for proponents of the invisible-hand justification to prove their case as it is for critics to disprove.

Given this inherent difficulty of direct access to the necessary evidence, proponents and critics fall back upon indirect strategies of assessment. For their part, critics examine the inputs into the competitive discovery procedure in order to indirectly impeach its outputs. A typical response to the informational argument for the adversary system, for example, is that it would be astonishing if the partisan motivations and rhetorical tricks of advocates tended to cancel each other out, rather than simply deepening the jury's confusion and thus tending to produce random or pernicious outcomes.[93]

The problem with such arguments is that all invisible-hand processes are astonishing,[94] in the sense that their inputs always seem disreputable taken in isolation. A narrow focus on the self-interested motivations and self-serving actions of individuals in local contexts will always make it seem surprising that the aggregation of individual motives and behaviors could produce social goods at the level of the overall system. That is the very point of invisible-hand justifications, their central alchemy. It is a straightforward fallacy of composition to assume that because market participants are self-interested, the market as a whole cannot serve the public interest, however defined. It is equally fallacious to assume that because advocates in jury trials use rhetorical tricks, the interaction of their efforts must simply sow more confusion.

Conversely, proponents of invisible-hand justifications attempt to offer indirect evidence for the epistemic success of competition by invoking mechanisms of evolution or social selection. On this sort of argument, the relevant institutions can be indirectly shown to produce better information by virtue of their competitive success in environments where more information is advantageous. Hayek, for example, fell back upon the following claim:

> When... we do not know in advance the facts we wish to discover with the help of competition, we are also unable to determine how effectively competition leads to the discovery of all the relevant circumstances that could have been discovered. All that can be empirically verified is that *societies making use of competition for this purpose realize this outcome to a greater extent than do others—a question which, it seems to me, the history of civilization answers emphatically in the affirmative.*[95]

Analogous arguments from competitive social selection are legion. Luther Gulick, an American official writing after the Second World War, suggested that the Allied democracies had emerged victorious over the Axis powers because the principle of free political speech had allowed democratic governments to learn from their mistakes and to correct their policies more quickly than could their enemies.[96] On a smaller institutional scale, Hayek also deployed social selection arguments for the common law, describing it as a spontaneous order that embodies more latent information than a centralized designer of rules could comprehend, and suggesting a competitive advantage for common-law legal systems.[97] Finally, an interesting variant is the argument that the adversary system of litigation and the inquisitorial system must be about equally good at producing truth: "it would be ... astounding to discover a great difference in veracity between the Anglo-American [adversarial] and Continental [inquisitorial] systems, for surely such a difference would after so many centuries have become a commonplace in our folklore."[98]

All of these arguments but the last, however, commit the fallacy of assuming that what is true of the whole must be true of the parts, taken one by one—the fallacy of division. Even if there is selection pressure at the level of *whole societies*, such pressure need not entail that some *subsystem* within a given society—the free market, freedom of political speech, the adversary system, or the common law—is superior to an alternative subsystem in other societies. Even if social selection exists, it operates on the society as a whole, as an integrated total system, and no inference about the parts follows.[99] Indeed, it might be that the subsystem that the analyst praises actually drags down the performance of the whole, but not so much as to exceed advantages on other margins.

Is the lesson of 1989 that free markets are superior to command-and-control economies, or that democratic political systems are superior to authoritarian ones? All that can be observed is that the *combination* of markets plus democracy is superior to the *combination* of command and control plus authoritarianism; disentangling the causal effect of each component requires further cases. "Although the Communist economies had planning but no markets, they also had political dictatorship, a background condition that any experimental designer would like to be able to alter."[100]

Likewise, it might be that the common law or the adversary system is a net cost, compared to the civil law and inquisitorial alternatives, but that societies that have the common law or the adversary system also tend to have other institutions that give them decisive advantages over competitors.[101] In the natural selection of biological organisms, the analogous phenomenon is pleiotropy, in which some genotype that produces both negative and positive phenotypic traits can survive and even spread when its benefits outweigh its costs.[102] That the package is optimal does not imply that all of its subparts are optimal or even beneficial, taken one by one.

The suggestion, then, is that the argument from competition as a discovery procedure yields claims that are both empirical and unverifiable; indirect strategies of assessment—examining inputs or appealing to social or institutional selection—cannot close the gap. We are left with another genuine dilemma, applicable to the subset of invisible-hand justifications that posit truth or information as the good produced as the unintended by-product of individual interaction.

SYSTEM EFFECTS AND THE INVISIBLE HAND

Invisible-hand justifications are a striking and important subclass of systemic analysis, and are ubiquitous in legal and political theory. My aim has been analytic, not substantive; not to issue judgments about the merits of such arguments, but to get clear about the conditions under which they might or might not hold. Where there is a well-defined substitute for or analogue to the price system of explicit markets, and where norms of altruism or general morality are unnecessary or positively harmful to the operation and stability of the system, invisible-hand justifications are most likely to be cogent, whether or not true or dispositive. More fundamentally, however, invisible-hand justifications face a set of recurring dilemmas that arise from the systemic character of their structure—dilemmas involving the lumpiness of norms, problems of partial compliance, and the difficulties of empirical but intrinsically unverifiable claims. Systemic analysis of legal and political institutions, especially constitutions, proceeds blindly if it fails to recognize these dilemmas.

CHAPTER 4

Systemic Feedback through Selection

S o far I have discussed, for the most part, synchronic system effects, in which the properties of a system differ from the properties of its components at a given time. This chapter explores diachronic system effects, in which institutions change over time as a consequence of changes in their memberships, and the overall constitutional system changes over time as a consequence of changes in its component institutions. Viewing system effects diachronically yields a dynamic perspective on constitutionalism.

Diachronic change in the constitutional system results, among other ways, from *selection effects*. Constitutional rules not only affect the incentives of the actors who happen to occupy official posts at any given time, but also affect which (potential) officials occupy those posts over time; put conversely, constitutional rules themselves help to construct the pool of potential and actual officeholders, as well as helping to determine the behavior of current officeholders. While an incentive analysis is short-term and static, asking only how legal rules affect the behavior of a given set of officeholders, a selection analysis is long-term and dynamic, asking how legal rules themselves produce systemic *feedback effects* that, over time, bring new types of government officials into power.[1] Feedback effects of this sort are a central tool of systems analysis.[2]

The precise nature of the feedback effects depends upon context. Some constitutional rules prove self-stabilizing: the rules tend to select a corps of officeholders who will act to uphold and stabilize the rules themselves. Other constitutional rules, by contrast, prove self-undermining: the rules tend to select a corps of officeholders who work to undermine or destabilize the rules themselves. This framework supplies insights into diverse areas of constitutional law and theory, including governmental structure, the eligibility, compensation, and immunity of officials, elections and voting rights, the national government's power to regulate commerce, and free speech and political association. Although the systemic analysis of selection effects is not wholly absent from constitutional theory, it is usually confined to particular debates on particular topics. My theoretical ambition here is to generalize the analysis of selection effects across constitutional contexts, and to elicit their systemic implications.

SELECTION EFFECTS: EXAMPLES AND MECHANISMS

To motivate the later discussion, I will begin with some concrete illustrations of selection effects. The most obvious setting—elections—comes first; less intuitive examples follow.

Elections. The election of federal officeholders is an obvious subject for selection analysis.[3] A simple criterion for evaluating such rules is whether they produce good officeholders, where "good" is defined according to some background normative theory of official performance. Thus Madison described elections, in part, as filtering devices:[4] elections would strain out bad characters and ensure that public-spirited citizens—a "natural aristocracy" of "virtue and talents"—would rise into government.[5]

A strictly incentive-based analysis describes elections, not as filtering devices, but instead as incentive devices: repeated elections reduce agency slack—the ability of self-interested officials to divert resources from the public welfare to personal gain—by forcing officeholders to adopt policies that accord with the preferences of electoral majorities, on pain of being turned out at the next election.[6] This is an application to elections of David Hume's knavery principle, which holds that "in contriving any system of government, and fixing the several checks and controuls of the constitution, every man ought to be supposed a *knave*, and to have no other end, in all his actions, than private interest."[7] On this view, all potential officeholders are assumed to be narrowly self-interested, and the constitutional problem is to turn self-interest to public advantage by suitable design of the electoral system. The filtering model, by contrast, posits that officials are motivationally heterogeneous. Candidates may have either good (public-spirited) or bad (narrowly self-interested) characters, and the constitutional problem is to design elections so as to enable voters to sort the one from the other.

In the strands of political science most heavily influenced by rational choice theory, the Humean approach is distilled in the median-voter model.[8] The simplest versions of the model show, under highly stylized assumptions, that where two self-interested political parties must bid for the electoral support of voters whose preferences are arrayed on a single dimension—say, from the leftmost voter, who prefers big government, to the rightmost voter, who prefers a minimalist libertarian state—the parties will both adopt platforms that maximally satisfy the preferences of the median voter.[9] Politicians here are ciphers, mere stand-ins for party platforms; their personal character is irrelevant.

Many features of ordinary electoral politics, however, cannot be explained by the median-voter model in any straightforward way, and are better explained by the filtering account. Voters often devote a great deal of attention to candidates' "character," valuing "principle" and "consistency" in public position-taking and private behavior; conversely, voters condemn "waffling" or "pandering" to the interests of electoral majorities. This is inexplicable on the median-voter model, in which encouraging candidates to pander to voters is the very point of the electoral exercise.[10] So an account that treats elections as filters for selecting good characters is, at least, a necessary supplement to incentive-based accounts that treat elections strictly as mechanisms for forcing accountability on uniformly self-interested politicians.

Official immunity. Under the quasi-constitutional law of official immunity, particular officeholders enjoy immunity against damages suits brought by citizens whose legal rights have been violated. Generally speaking, legislators, judges, and prosecutors enjoy absolute immunity for conduct within the "outer perimeter" of their official duties, as does the president, while subordinate executive officials enjoy only qualified immunity, which applies whenever the official acts in "objective good faith"—that is, unless the official violated the plaintiff's "clearly established" rights.[11] Official immunity is often justified by a simple incentive story: "fear of being sued will dampen the ardor of all but the most resolute, or the most irresponsible [public officials], in the discharge of their duties."[12] The implicit logic here is that the threat of liability imposes expected pecuniary costs, in the form of damages and litigation expenses arising from official actions. There is also a nonpecuniary cost: litigation diverts officials from their duties, and if those officials enjoy the duties attached to the office more than participating in litigation, then the diversion reduces the official's nonpecuniary compensation as well. On this picture, immunity supplies an incentive for vigorous activity that existing officials would otherwise fail to supply—although the Supreme Court has never quite explained why the deterrent threat of liability will be excessive, rather than optimal.

An argument from selection effects complements, and complicates, the incentive-based account. Absent official immunity, the threat of citizen lawsuits might change not only the behavior of existing officials, but also the mix of persons who seek or accept office over time. The Supreme Court has assumed that the change would be for the worse, so that the absence of qualified immunity would "deter[ ] able citizens from acceptance of public office."[13] Here the Court's logic supposes that the most able candidates for office will anticipate the threat of liability and will, at the margin, substitute activities with lower expected costs, such as private-sector work. The remaining candidates in the pool will be those whose next-best opportunity in the private sector provides less total compensation than federal office, even given the additional expected costs of litigation. Those candidates will tend to be less able, all else equal; that is why their private-sector opportunities are still less attractive than a federal post shadowed by the threat of litigation.

There are many contestable assumptions here, about the information and rational expectations of potential candidates for federal office, and about the efficiency of the background labor markets that set the value of candidates' next-best opportunities. Even granting all those assumptions, however, it is not clear that the absence of official immunity would, on net, reduce the quality of the pool of candidates for federal offices. An alternative possibility is that the absence of immunity would provide a useful screening or sorting mechanism that separates good or public-spirited officials from bad or ill-motivated officials.

The screening story would run like this. Suppose that the pool of candidates for federal offices generally contains two types. A-type candidates are public-spirited, in the sense that they are respectful of citizens' legal rights and have no desire to violate them. B-type candidates are ill-motivated, in the sense that they lack any respect for citizens' legal rights. Each candidate possesses private information—that is, information known only to the candidate, not to others—about which type she is. In this situation, B-types will claim to be A-types; doing so is costless, while admitting (to the voters or officials who are electing or appointing them) that they are B-types would be disqualifying.

Some mechanism is needed to screen or sort good A-types from bad B-types, and liability for official actions can do the trick. The prospect of liability for violating citizens' rights is differentially costly to the two types of candidates: A-types, who know that they will rarely violate rights, will also know that their expected liability costs are very low; B-types will correctly expect that their liability costs will be high. All else equal, then, A-types will tend to apply for positions that lack official immunity more than B-types will. To be sure, courts will sometimes err, deciding that even an A-type official has violated rights, or deciding that a B-type official has not. But unless courts are wholly random, the absence of immunity will tend to push A-types toward the office and B-types away from it. Given this, the law should not recognize official immunity; its absence is a useful screening mechanism for identifying rights-respecting applicants.

It is irrelevant whether this screening argument is persuasive, on the merits. The lens of selection effects brings into focus a theoretically crucial argument against official immunity, an argument that is invisible within the standard analysis of immunity's incentive effects.

The Compensation Clauses. The Compensation Clause of Article III provides that the judges shall, "at stated Times, receive for their Services, a Compensation, which shall not be diminished during their Continuance in Office."[14] Article II contains a similar, although not strictly parallel, clause: the president "shall, at stated Times, receive for his services, a Compensation, which shall neither be encreased nor diminished during the Period for which he shall have been elected."[15] The difference here is that the judges' salaries may be increased during their term in office—a term consisting of life tenure—while the president's may not.

The standard account of these clauses points to their effects on the incentives of current officeholders. In Hamilton's words, "a power over a man's subsistence amounts to a power over his will."[16] The Compensation Clauses thus promote executive and judicial independence from legislative bullying. On this account, the Constitutional Convention traded off an increased risk of congressional influence over the judges, through salary increases, in order to make it possible for Congress to raise judicial salaries during the judges' life terms. To protect the judicial process by barring congressional bribes would have the side effect of barring pay raises during the whole term of a judge's service. The president, unlike the judges, serves only a four-year term. So this side effect is much less important in the presidential setting, and the Article II rules bar presidential salary increases.

To this standard account, however, we may juxtapose a selection-effects analysis. In the Article III setting, one idea is that the that the clause not only secures judicial independence, but helps to "induce 'learned' men and women 'to quit the lucrative pursuits' of the private sector."[17] We may interpret this as a concern about the selection effects of the Compensation Clause. The constitutional rules affect the composition of the pool of lawyers from which candidates for federal judicial service are drawn, because possible candidates know the rules and select in or out of the pool according to the relative costs and benefits of judicial service and private-sector opportunities. The Supreme Court has said that the guarantee against salary reduction "ensures a prospective judge that...the compensation of the new post will not diminish."[18] The salary stability provided by the clause is thus a benefit that, at the margin, encourages high-value lawyers whose compensation is far more variable to forego private-sector opportunities.[19]

A contrary view, however, is that keeping explicit judicial compensation lower than in comparable private-sector opportunities will tend to select for those who enjoy the job for its own sake, rather than instrumentally. The judge who derives satisfaction from performing the job enjoys a stream of nonpecuniary income; lowering pecuniary income tends to select candidates who derive intrinsic satisfaction from the work. And those candidates (the argument might run) will be better, on some normative account of good judging, than candidates for whom pecuniary compensation is the most important element of the overall mix. We need not attempt to arbitrate between these competing views here. The important point, one to which I return below, is that the clause's second-order effects on the pool of potential federal judges operate through effects on both pecuniary and nonpecuniary compensation.

The Ascertainment Clause. The Ascertainment Clause is the basic provision for congressional salaries; it states that "[t]he Senators and Representatives shall receive a Compensation for their Services, to be ascertained by Law, and paid out of the Treasury of the United States."[20] Two incentive stories are relevant here. First, as to the source of the payment, many delegates to the constitutional convention hoped that requiring federal legislators to be paid according to federal law and out of federal funds—rather than state funds, the practice under the Articles of Confederation—would make them less beholden to state governments.[21] Second, as to the fact of payment, the convention feared that unpaid legislators would turn to corruption to supplement their incomes. As Story put it, "they might be compelled by their necessities, or tempted by their wants, to yield up their independence, and perhaps their integrity, to the allurements of the corrupt, or the opulent."[22]

The latter account posits a given, preselected group of unpaid legislators and asks how the presence or absence of compensation will affect their behavior. Against this we may juxtapose an account that looks to the selection effects of legislative compensation. On this view, high salaries will attract especially venal candidates to office, plausibly increasing rather than decreasing the incidence of corruption. No salaries, or nominal salaries, would instead differentially select for candidates who derive intrinsic satisfaction—and thus a stream of nonpecuniary income—from the position. Such officials will, on this view, outperform officials who hold the job for its accompanying salary. A long tradition, traceable at least to country-party critiques of the English royal court, condemns the latter sort of officeholder as corrupt "placemen."[23]

This argument from selection effects, however, is ambiguous in its turn. Supporters of the federal legislative salary argued that providing no salary would not select for candidates motivated by intrinsic enjoyment of the office, but would instead simply select for wealthy candidates, creating a de facto legislative plutocracy. A few opponents of the federal legislative salary accepted this causal account, but claimed that the tendency to select for wealthy legislators would be good rather than bad, at least as to the Senate. As Charles Cotesworth Pinckney argued at the convention, "As this (the Senatorial) branch was meant to represent the wealth of the Country, it ought to be composed of persons of wealth; and if no allowance was to be made the wealthy alone would undertake the service."[24]

The structure of this debate is parallel to the debate over judicial compensation. In both the judicial and legislative settings, two opposing selection arguments might be advanced. Proponents of high official salaries fear that low compensation will produce a cohort of insufficiently talented, and excessively wealthy, amateur enthusiasts. Opponents of high official salaries fear that high compensation will produce a cohort of talented but venal opportunists. This debate is partly empirical—what exactly will the selection effects of various salary levels be?—and partly normative—will the selection effects produce good or bad officials (given some background normative theory)? For present purposes, however, the debate need not be resolved. The point that matters here is that a selection account reframes the analysis based solely on incentives.

SELECTION MECHANISMS: A TAXONOMY

In these and other cases, how do legal rules affect the selection of public officeholders and other actors over time? Here I will offer a number of conceptual distinctions, in order to develop a taxonomy of selection mechanisms, and in order to prepare the ground for an analysis of the long-run systemic consequences of selection.

Selection of whom by whom? Selection-based accounts necessarily suppose that a smaller group is selected, by some agent, from a larger group. Either the selecting agent or the selected group varies across cases. To illustrate variation in the selecting agent, we may consider the standard case in which holders of public office are selected from a pool of candidates. The selecting agent may be another public official or set of officials, as when the president appoints federal judges with Senate consent, or it may be the voters, as in the selection between or among candidates for the presidency itself. To illustrate variation in the selected group, we may consider the difference between legal rules that (1) select public officeholders from a pool of candidates or (2) select voters from a pool of citizens. Although the examples above all involve the selection of officeholders, the analysis extends straightforwardly to rules that allocate the voting franchise among citizens, such as state electoral laws and the Voting Rights Act; I will offer some illustrations shortly. In principle other variants exist, although I shall not examine them; for example, legal rules enacted by voters and their official representatives select citizens from the broader pool of residents and select residents from the broader pool of would-be immigrants.

Direct versus indirect selection effects. Selection effects may operate directly or indirectly. Direct selection effects flow from rules that themselves establish or structure processes for selecting federal officers. Obvious examples in this category include the Qualifications Clauses of Articles I and II, which set age, residency, and citizenship requirements for federal legislative and executive office;[25] the rules in Article II and the Twelfth Amendment for electing presidents;[26] and the Appointments Clause of Article II, which specifies processes for the selection of federal executive and judicial officers.[27] But rules that do not in explicit terms address the selection of officeholders can have important indirect selection effects. Consider the examples of official immunity, the Compensation Clauses, and the Ascertainment Clause, all of which generate indirect selection effects as a consequence of their direct effects on the compensation of officeholders.

Indirect Selection Effects: Three Mechanisms

The incentive accounts sampled above share three consequential assumptions. (1) The set of officeholders is taken to be fixed. Selection takes place offstage; the only question is to design incentives for given officeholders. (2) All officeholders are assumed to be rationally self-interested, and thus motivationally homogeneous. (3) The motivations of officeholders are assumed to be not only homogenous, but wholly exogenous to the selection process; motivations are not affected by the process of selection to office.

I will proceed by relaxing each of these assumptions in succession and cumulatively. This procedure generates three different selection mechanisms: changes in the *relative costs* of officeholding; *screening* or sorting good types from bad types; and the *causal aftereffects* of selection rules. These mechanisms in turn generate new hypotheses or normative accounts in various areas of constitutional law and theory.

Relative costs. Relaxing the first assumption, but retaining the other two, we say that all actors have uniformly self-interested and selection-independent preferences, but that the pool of officeholders changes over time depending on the costs and benefits of officeholding. Constitutional rules that structure the incentives of current officers also alter the costs and benefits facing potential or prospective holders of federal offices when deciding whether to pursue or accept an office, or deciding, at an earlier stage, to invest in the necessary qualifications for particular federal offices. Incentive rules governing current officeholders impose costs and benefits upon those whose behavior is shaped by the incentives, but those costs also affect the expectations of potential officeholders about the attractiveness of holding a given position, relative to other employment the potential officeholder might obtain or other courses of action she might pursue. To be clear, the relative-cost mechanism retains the assumption that the pool of potential candidates for office is motivationally homogeneous: every agent attempts to maximize total compensation by choosing the available employment that brings the greatest returns. The distinctive contribution of the relative-cost mechanism is just to drive the analysis back to the earlier point at which rational potential candidates assess the costs and benefits of officeholding.

Compensation can take many forms, of which cash salary is only one. A given position may also yield a stream of implicit (or nonpecuniary, or in-kind) compensation, in the form of inherent interest, the opportunity to promote the officeholder's vision of good government, prestige, power, leisure, or any number of other goods. In many cases, the implicit elements of compensation may dwarf the explicit ones; it is unlikely that the pool of candidates for president would be greatly affected, all else equal, if the presidential salary were cut in half. This is so not because presidents can borrow against expected future income—a practice that raises many complex legal questions,[28] and that brings political costs— but because the nominal salary is dominated by the in-kind compensation, in the form of power and prestige, that the office confers.

Constitutional rules that shape the incentives of current office-holders may thus have critical selection effects by affecting either pecuniary or nonpecuniary compensation. Collating this with the earlier distinction between direct and indirect effects yields a four-square taxonomy: constitutional rules may have (1) direct effects on pecuniary compensation, (2) indirect effects on pecuniary compensation, (3) direct effects on nonpecuniary compensation, or (4) indirect effects on nonpecuniary compensation. Case (1) is exemplified by the Article I rule prohibiting federal officers from accepting "emoluments" from foreign states; case (2) is exemplified by the Ascertainment and Compensation Clauses, to which I shall return below; case (3) is exemplified by the prohibition on federal officers accepting titles of nobility from foreign governments, and the broader prohibition on the issuance on titles of nobility by the federal government (either to officers or citizens);[29] and case (4) is exemplified by the argument, mentioned above, that official immunity indirectly prevents the reduction in nonpecuniary compensations that arises when office-holders are constantly exposed to the threat of lawsuits.

The important point, however, is just that in every case it is the net system-level effect of the relevant constitutional rule that matters. Every office carries a mix of pecuniary income or salary and nonpecuniary compensation; by changing the level or character of one or the other of these elements of total compensation, constitutional rules can change the total mix of compensation and thus change the pool of candidates who will find the office more attractive than other opportunities.

Screening mechanisms. Relaxing the first two assumptions, but retaining the third, we stipulate both that the pool of potential officeholders changes over time, and that the pool is motivationally heterogeneous rather than homogeneous. We assume, in other words, that the pool of candidates is composed of two different types, one of which will perform better in the office than the other, according to whatever normative theory of government we assume. Candidates know their own types, but this information is private, and cannot be directly observed by the officials who appoint them or by voters who elect them. In these circumstances, bad types will mimic good types, saying all the right things so long as it is costless to do so. The problem then becomes one of sorting good types from apparently identical bad types.

In many circumstances, institutions cope with this problem by adopting screening mechanisms.[30] The core idea is to adopt some prerequisites or conditions for obtaining whatever benefit the institution supplies; the prerequisite must provide differential advantages to good types or impose differential costs upon bad types. Even though the institutional designer cannot directly observe candidates' types, good and bad types will then sort themselves appropriately; at the margin, good types will tend to accept the benefit with the conditions, while bad types will tend to decline the benefit by going elsewhere. The differential benefit thus screens the good from the bad. For a simple example, consider a health insurance company that offers significantly lower benefits in the early period of a contract; this makes the contract less attractive to individuals who suffer preexisting conditions, or who anticipate imminent illness. Those types will tend to select themselves out of the insurance pool, to the benefit of healthy policyholders who would otherwise pay higher premiums to cover the expenses of the ill.[31] Constitutional designers might adopt similar screening mechanisms that attempt to sort agents with desirable motivations from agents with undesirable ones.

Causal aftereffects. Relaxing all three assumptions, we stipulate that the pool of officeholders changes over time, that officials' motivations are heterogeneous, and that those motivations are at least in part an endogenous product of the selection process. To the extent motivations determine behavior, this means that the selection procedure can itself affect the future behavior of officeholders—not merely ex ante, by altering the relative costs of officeholding and thus the ex ante willingness of the marginal candidate to accept office, but instead by changing the ex post utility the officeholder derives from being selected or by changing the officeholder's conception of the role she is to fill. The behavior of current officeholders is shaped, not by the anticipation of rewards and penalties for future action, but by the selection process through which the officeholder previously attained her post.

A prominent example in this category involves "precommitment politics"[32]—the possibility that candidates for elected office, or nominees for appointed office, will make promises to the electorates, presidents, senators, or other actors who have the power to elect, nominate, or confirm them. Presidential candidates promise "no new taxes"; nominees for judgeships commit to respecting *Roe v. Wade*[33] as settled law. The motive for the promise is to gain the post, but the making of the promise can itself affect the behavior of the officeholders who are eventually elected or selected. Once in power, the officeholder may adhere to the promise because it was previously made, even if the officeholder now thinks (or always thought) that the promised policy is a bad one.

This ex post effect of the selection process can arise in two ways. First, the officeholder might foresee a reputational cost to promise-breaking, especially if the officeholder must eventually undergo reelection or renomination, and will thus have to obtain the approval of the same body to which the (broken) promise was initially made.

In this case, the causal aftereffect is reducible to an incentive effect—a product of the officeholder's forward-looking concern for reelection. But the reputational cost may be positive even if the officeholder cannot run again—second-term presidents are said to care deeply about their reputations.[34] Second, and more interestingly, the officeholder might internalize the promise made to gain office; it might become a part of her self-conception, or her conception of the role she now fills, that her public promises should be honored. In that case the selection process has produced a genuine causal aftereffect, one that is not reducible to an incentive-based account.

Putting aside incentives, we may in some cases parsimoniously attempt to reduce causal aftereffects to some other selection mechanism, either a relative-cost mechanism or a screening mechanism. To a pro-life lawyer, the political necessity to promise to respect *Roe* reduces the expected utility of holding a judgeship, if the lawyer would otherwise hope to use the office to satisfy his ideological agenda, and this induces self-selection away from a judicial career. Likewise, the need to publicly commit to a constitutionally dubious decision might function as a screening mechanism that sorts judicial nominees who respect precedent from those who do not. In other cases, however, the causal aftereffect seems irreducible.

SELECTION AND SYSTEMIC FEEDBACK

I am now in position to pursue my major claim: selection effects drive the dynamics of the constitutional system. Over time, selection effects will produce *systemic feedback*: rules that affect selection might tend either to stabilize or to undermine the rules themselves. In the stabilizing case, constitutional rules tend to select for officeholders who will respect, enforce, and help to entrench the rules. In the undermining case, constitutional rules select for officeholders who work to negate, contract, expand, or otherwise alter the rules.

The stability of constitutional rules may be examined at higher or lower levels of generality, and in a shorter or longer time frame. As to the first distinction, constitutional stability may be examined either at the macrolevel of the whole constitution, or at the microlevel of particular provisions. Even where the macrostructure of a constitution is recognizably stable over time, particular provisions may contract, expand, or be reinterpreted under a variety of political and social pressures. The United States Constitution is an example of this phenomenon. Although today's Constitution is a recognizable descendent of the Constitution of the founding, in the sense that basic features like bicameralism, federalism, and an independently elected executive are still in place, some provisions have more or less disappeared (for example, the Contracts Clause) while others have assumed ever-larger importance (for example, free speech). Not all of these changes, of course, can be explained by selection effects; below I will indicate some cases in which selection-based explanations seem particularly apt.

As to the second distinction, constitutional structures or provisions may be stable in the short run but not in the long run. An example I will take up below involves the Commerce Clause and the general scope of enumerated federal legislative powers, which expanded far more rapidly in the Constitution's second century than in its first.[35] Less intuitively, structures and provisions can instead be unstable in the short run while stable in the long run, as I also illustrate below.

SELF-STABILIZING CONSTITUTIONAL RULES

I will begin with the case of self-stabilizing rules, and then turn to self-undermining ones.

Voting rights. Constitutional rules may stabilize themselves by affecting the composition of the pool of candidates for elected offices. Consider the various constitutional rules that have, at various points in American history, expanded the franchise to new individuals and groups. Examples here are the Fifteenth and Nineteenth Amendments, and even the Voting Rights Act of 1965, if we accept the widespread view that the act has some form of quasi-constitutional stature.[36]

A standard view holds that franchise-expanding rules of this sort are extremely stable; once granted, they are almost never revoked. This view must be qualified in light of recent work on the history of American voting rights, showing important contractions of the franchise in the late nineteenth and early twentieth centuries.[37] At a higher level of abstraction, however, it seems clear that liberal democracies have universally pushed toward universal suffrage. In the broad, any expansion of voting rights tends to show a certain stickiness, creating a ratchet effect over time.

Two selection mechanisms help to explain this effect. First, at the de jure level of formal voting rights, is the effect of selection into the pool of actual voters. The franchise-expanding rule will necessarily tend to increase the fraction of actual voters from the relevant group, and those voters are most unlikely ever to vote for a repeal of their own voting rights.[38] Second, at the de facto level of effective voting power, the franchise-expanding rule will tend to increase the election or selection of officials from the newly enfranchised group, and those officials will resist any repeal or dilution of the electoral clout of the group from which they are drawn. The second effect may, however, be diluted by agency slack between the group and the officials drawn from the group. A legislator elected by and from a minority group might resist a plan to redraw a majority-minority voting district, even if spreading minority voters out over a larger number of districts might maximize the minority's overall influence upon legislators drawn from the majority group.[39]

In these cases the selection effect does not operate by altering the net benefits of officeholding. We may stipulate that the total package of explicit and implicit compensation for the relevant post remains unchanged. Instead the selection effect alters the prior likelihood that the relevant candidates can attain the posts they seek. The presence of a larger number of voters from the relevant group in the voting pool encourages members of that group to enter the candidate pool.

These selection effects do not guarantee political change. First, within particular groups, a large fraction of those holding the legal right to vote may choose not to exercise it. Second, the relevant constitutional rules may go unenforced in the period before the new cohort of officials has come into office; of course the history of black voting rights between 1870 (the enactment of the Fifteenth Amendment) and the 1965 Voting Rights Act is a notorious example of the latter possibility, as black voting rights were systematically denied or evaded by white officials in (mostly) southern states.[40] But that is just to say that as a practical matter the franchise-expanding rule does not exist until it is genuinely enforced. Once enforcement is real, the rule becomes self-stabilizing as officials from the newly enfranchised group enter the system. Thus the Voting Rights Act has itself helped to produce a cohort of black officials in both federal and state governments who vigorously resist any contraction or dilution of black voting rights.

Qualifications for office. Articles I and II enact mandatory age, citizenship, and residence requirements for federal legislative and executive office, respectively.[41] It is trivial that those requirements have direct selection effects. A harder question is whether the requirements have indirect selection effects that are either self-stabilizing or self-undermining. The answer plausibly turns on the details of the way the rules are cast.

For simplicity, consider the age minimums for federal office—twenty-five for the House, thirty for the Senate, thirty-five for the presidency. Any officers selected under these rules will be older than the age minimum, and would thus have no interest in destabilizing the rules; should legislators, for example, approve a constitutional amendment lowering the age minimums, the principal effect would simply be to expand the pool of potential challengers for the legislators' offices. Suppose, however, that the framers had also included mandatory age maximums for federal office—perhaps on the same theory that drives mandatory retirement ages for various professions. A plausible prediction is that mandatory maximums would prove chronically unstable. The effect of the rules would be to select for officials whose position would be increasingly threatened by the rules as the officials acquire more seniority. With an age maximum of seventy, we should be unsurprised to find powerful sixty-nine-year-old legislators working toward repeal of the rule or attempting to undermine it in more subtle ways.

A similar analysis suggests that term limits will be subject to constant pressure from senior officials who wish to undermine the limits themselves. So far the empirical evidence is mixed. Although the federal Constitution contains no legislative term limits, and states are constitutionally barred from adding federal term limits,[42] the House imposed a term limit on committee chairs by intracameral rule in 1995, while the Senate Republican conference adopted an internal equivalent in 1996;[43] the Twenty-second Amendment, adopted in 1951, imposes a two-term limitation on the presidency.[44] The latter rule was made necessary by Roosevelt's decision to flout an unwritten norm dating from Washington's presidency. Although the written rule has proved more stable, it is striking that many recent two-term incumbents have floated proposals for its repeal or modification.[45] Congressional committee term limits, it appears, have been less stable. In 2003, senior Republican senators diluted their conference's rule through narrow interpretation just before it threatened to strip them of their preferred committee chairs.[46] In 2009, the Democratic House majority ended the six-year term limit for committee chairs, rolling back the 1995 rule completely.[47]

The Ascertainment Clause (redux). Let us revisit the constitutional rules governing official salaries. The simplest of those rules—the decision embodied in the Ascertainment Clause to pay federal legislators something rather than nothing—plausibly has self-stabilizing effects. The basic theory of the clause, that a salary will attract well-qualified and (therefore) well-motivated legislators to office, ensures that those legislators will act to protect the rule against later amendment or circumvention. If the clause's theory is correct, then the clause itself represents good policy and will be protected against change by the well-motivated legislators the clause effectively selects. The converse does not hold, however. The clause may be self-stabilizing even if guaranteed salaries merely attract venal candidates to office (as opponents of the clause argued).[48] In that case the clause is a bad policy, but nonetheless a self-stabilizing one: venal legislators will be as assiduous as well-motivated legislators in protecting the clause from amendment or circumvention, precisely because the clause is what allows venal legislators to feed at the public trough. The example again emphasizes that either good or bad rules may be self-stabilizing.

Free speech (and a free press). Consider a crude account of the institutional dynamics of constitutional free-speech law, particularly the law bearing on the speech rights of media defendants (such as the restrictive tests for defamation of public officials and public figures, restrictive rules about licensing, censorship and prior restraints, and the general precept that governmental regulation must be content-neutral). On this account, the justices of the Supreme Court are particularly susceptible to informal suasion, flattery, or criticism from media organs with a vested interest in protecting and expanding speech rights. Justices who issue speech-protective decisions are praised for their wisdom and respect for precedent by elements of the large institutional media.[49] Justices who attempt to restrict media prerogatives are condemned as extremist or lawless.[50] Over time, then, the justices strongly protect media interests.

This account has too many moving parts and contestable assumptions to be plausible on its own terms. "The media" is not a natural kind; it is an internally heterogeneous collection of competing economic structures and interests. And the account assumes that the judicial maximand is reputation among the elites who consume the product of the institutional media—merely one possible answer to the notoriously complex question about what judges, or Supreme Court justices, maximize.[51] Most crucially, the implicit claim here is strictly one about the incentives of sitting justices, who are assumed to move in the direction of media preferences. An awkward fact for this account is the consistent finding, in empirical political science, that there is a strong correlation between the justices' ideological values *at the time of nomination* and their subsequent votes in civil liberties cases, including free-speech cases.[52] If this is so, then justices do not seem to move in the direction of media preferences after taking the bench. (Nor does it seem plausible to think that the incentive effect operates on lower-court judges, from whose ranks most justices are now drawn; lower-court judges do not predictably receive a great deal of public attention.)

But this critique itself suggests an improved version of the general account, based on selection rather than incentives. In political science, attitudinal scholarship attempts to gauge justices' ideology at the time of nomination by the party of the appointing president and, critically, by editorials written at the time of nomination in the major national newspapers,[53] who tend to praise nominees with strong free-speech proclivities. Suppose that those proclivities are themselves wholly exogenous, not at all the product of media pressure. Even if they are, to the extent that the anticipated reaction of the press influences presidential selection of Supreme Court nominees—and there is every reason to think that the press's influence is very real[54]—then the selection of nominees will be skewed in the direction of nominees who support media free-speech claims. The other weaknesses of the account remain, but the selection lens at least makes the picture of systematic press influence on the Supreme Court seem more plausible than it otherwise would.

SELF-UNDERMINING CONSTITUTIONAL RULES

I now turn to constitutional rules whose selection effects destabilize or undermine the rules themselves. Two preliminary points are necessary. First, as before, no normative connotation should be attached to the positive claim that a given constitutional rule has self-undermining selection effects. Although this will in some cases be bad, perhaps because the systemic benefits of stability are particularly high in the relevant setting, in other cases destabilizing selection effects will prove beneficial. If a policy is desirable in the short run but undesirable in the long run, the destabilizing long-run selection effects of the policy may function as a built-in sunset provision or termination mechanism. Second, it is a mistake to assume that rules whose selection effects are self-undermining necessarily become *narrower* over time (or disappear entirely). In some cases, destabilizing selection effects can cause a broadening of the rules over time; the Commerce Clause illustrates this trend, as discussed below. The rule is nonetheless destabilized, in the sense that selection effects cause its original scope to change over time.

The Article III Compensation Clause (redux). Above, I suggested that the Ascertainment Clause is a simple example of a self-stabilizing rule.

Not so the Article III Compensation Clause. That clause is a ratchet-type rule: it authorizes Congress to set judicial salaries, and allows future increases, but forbids Congress to reduce salaries once they are set. Here the dynamic, over time, has been that Congress has systematically failed to provide judicial salary increases sufficient to keep pace with inflation.[55] Two forces drive this dynamic. First, Congress has often linked legislative salaries to judicial salaries, refusing to raise one unless both are raised. The heavy political pressure against legislative salary increases then keeps downward pressure on judicial salaries as well. Second, legislators understand the structure of the Compensation Clause as well as anyone else, and anticipate that any salary increase for the judges will be frozen into place by force of constitutional law. The predictable equilibrium reaction, one the framers ought themselves to have anticipated but failed to, is that Congress is more reluctant to raise judicial salaries in the first instance.

The result of these political forces is that the clause has a self-negating effect. As we have seen, a principal theory of the Article III Compensation Clause is that the ratchet-like protection against salary reduction would attract talented judges to office, "induc[ing] 'learned' men and women 'to quit the lucrative pursuits' of the private sector."[56] The guarantee "ensures a prospective judge that…the compensation of the new post will not diminish."[57] But the theory is flawed. It fails to take into account that Congress, like prospective judges, can anticipate the effects of the clause's structure. Legislators who anticipate the ratchet effect of any future increase will award fewer increases. The result is that the structure of the clause has perverse unanticipated consequences, and those consequences undermine or negate the personnel rationale that (in part) justified the clause's ratchet-like structure in the first place. Because Congress refuses to award judicial salary increases sufficient to keep pace with inflation, real judicial salaries decline, judges leave the bench,[58] and talented lawyers decline to serve as judges.[59] These effects occur at the margin, but they are hardly marginal; commentators increasingly describe the law of judicial compensation as a system in crisis.[60]

Commerce and enumeration. In principle, a constitutional rule might produce self-negating selection effects that either contract the scope of the rule or that expand it. Here I will offer a speculative account of the commerce power, and more generally the enumerated powers of the federal legislature, in which the effect is one of expansion. The basic idea here is that selection effects might reinforce, or accelerate, the expansion of the federal government's constitutional powers, and in this sense undermine or negate the original constitutional structure.

The background here is an implausible story about incentives. A rhetorical trope of federalist theory is the idea that "Congress" seeks to "aggrandize itself" at the expense of the states, swallowing ever-larger increments of power by pressing outward the boundaries of its enumerated powers with the acquiescence of compliant courts. But, as the scare quotes indicate, the story anthropomorphizes a collective institution. "Congress" cannot benefit from the increasing scope of enumerated powers, because Congress is merely an institutional label for a set of individuals who act through elaborate internal rules of procedure. Any account that posits a systematic tendency of Congress to attempt to expand its enumerated powers, over time, must be supplied with microfoundations in the behavior of the individuals who occupy the institution at different times.[61]

Selection analysis can fill in the critical gaps in the story of federal legislative aggrandizement. The key mechanism here involves changes, over time, in the benefits and costs to individuals of holding federal legislative office. I will not pretend to offer an historical account, but merely a stylized sketch to generate a hypothesis. Suppose that just after the founding era federal legislative service was seen as less prestigious than service in state government, in part because the powers of the federal government were far narrower than they are today. This state of affairs would produce self-stabilizing selection effects: holding other factors constant, federal legislative service would tend to attract legislators for whom substantive authority over policy questions was not a large element of implicit compensation.

Now suppose that some exogenous shock destabilizes the system, producing a broad consensus that the scope of congressional power must be increased to cope with new political, economic, or social problems. Perhaps the need for internal improvements, or the Civil War, or the growth of interstate railroads, produces a critical mass of states and individuals willing to turn to federal legislation for collective solutions.[62] Service in Congress would then have become relatively more attractive for legislators who derive enjoyment—implicit compensation—from holding authority or power over large questions of national policy. Once in place, such legislators might be expected to press the boundaries of the enumerated powers in new, more expansive directions. The point here is not, as in the aggrandizement story, that the new legislators desire to maximize the power of Congress as an institution; they strictly desire to maximize their own power, from which they derive implicit compensation. Maximizing legislators' own power, however, requires maximizing the power of Congress, because an individual federal legislator holds power strictly in proportion to her fractional share in the power of Congress as an institution.

This story is only partially sketched, and is speculative in the extreme. To test it, further specification would be required, as well as a great deal of careful historical work; the key question would be whether the historical break-points indicated above have indeed been associated with changes, over time, in the composition of the federal legislative corps, including the legislators' socioeconomic and professional backgrounds. Here too the cash value of selection analysis is to suggest new empirical hypotheses, ones that an exclusive focus on incentive-based accounts would obscure.

Tolerating the intolerant. A final example is the broadest so far. Here the possibility is that, under certain (possibly rare) political and social circumstances, the whole complex of constitutional rules that require toleration of the intolerant might have self-negating selection effects.

Roughly speaking, rules that require toleration of the intolerant are constitutional rules that require liberal democratic governments to extend rights of political speech, association, and participation, including voting, to illiberal individuals or groups whose professed ideals themselves reject toleration. Such groups would deny to other groups the very speech rights, and political rights, that the illiberal groups enjoy. Toleration of the intolerant is conventionally justified by a skeptical account of the incentives and motivations of the government officials who hold power in a liberal democratic regime. Those officials will tend, the story runs, to appease majority coalitions in the electorate by suppressing the speech of unpopular groups whose speech may make a valuable contribution to the marketplace of political ideas, even or especially if that speech is false or objectionable.

From the selection standpoint, however, this incentive-based justification for tolerating the intolerant is fatally static. The incentive-based justification overlooks a dynamic concern: tolerating the intolerant will bring to power officials, eventually including appointed judges, who may act intolerantly. In its most extreme version, the concern is that liberal democracy, with unrestricted rights of speech and democratic participation for illiberal groups, may prove self-negating or self-undermining: illiberal groups will use elections to seize control of the state and then entrench their intolerant policies, irrevocably revoking the speech rights, and democratic franchise, of the supporters of the former liberal regime.

The concern is a real one. Important cases of illiberal groups who have pursued this aim—seizing power through elections and turning it to illiberal or undemocratic ends—have been various Marxist, communist, and socialist parties committed to the abolition of bourgeois democracy; fascist groups committed to the same aim, although for nationalist rather than egalitarian reasons; and, especially, religious extremists who aim to abolish liberal democracy in favor of (some particular brand of) theocracy.[63] Indeed, a useful generalization from comparative politics is that the trend in the twentieth century was for illiberal groups to eschew violent revolution, in favor of an indirect strategy of undermining liberal democracy through the exercise of liberal democratic rights.[64] An ambiguous case is Hitler's seizure of power after the Nazi party's successes in the elections of 1933;[65] clearer, and more recent, cases involve theocratic Islamist parties in Algeria and other nations.[66]

The most stringent conceptions of free speech accept this dynamic possibility with equanimity, or at least resignation. As Justice Holmes put it, "[I]f, in the long run, the beliefs expressed in the proletarian dictatorship are destined to be accepted by the dominant forces of the community, the only meaning of free speech is that they should be given their chance and have their way."[67] There is a paradox implicit in Holmes's remark, however. A commitment to free speech and liberal democracy in the long run will short-circuit if it permits illiberal and antidemocratic forces to seize power in the short run, at some given moment.

On a different conception of free speech, therefore, the commitment to sustaining liberal democracy, over time, is taken to trump the commitment to respecting the liberal rights of illiberal groups, at any particular time. Although Holmes's position suggests that "the First Amendment places out of bounds any law that attempts to freeze public debate at a particular moment in time,"[68] the competing conception holds that public debate may legitimately be frozen, by coercive laws, on the question of the desirability of liberal democracy itself. Governments may structure the political process to exclude groups, movements, and parties who will not credibly commit to playing by the rules of the democratic game, not only in the current period but in future periods as well.

The latter position, rather than Holmes's pose of utter self-abnegation, has prevailed in most liberal democracies. Established democracies typically proscribe or prohibit antidemocratic parties, although the mechanics and scope of these proscriptions vary. The German Basic Law provides that "[p]arties which, by reason of their aims or the behavior of their adherents, seek to impair or abolish the free democratic basic order or to endanger the existence of the Federal Republic of Germany, shall be unconstitutional"; in other nations, constitutional provisions or statutes may vaguely commit all parties to "respect" for democracy, or may proscribe particular parties with historical resonance (such as the Italian Fascists).[69] In the German case, and in some others, a party may suffer proscription merely for advocating totalitarianism, while under current American law the government must prove advocacy that is likely to incite or produce imminent lawless action.[70] Whatever its normative merits as an aspirational ideal, however, the current test does not reflect the historical scope of American law, which has permitted proscription of antidemocratic parties ranging from former Confederate rebels to twentieth-century communists.[71]

The hard questions surrounding such laws are not ones of political theory, but rather of political strategy and tactics. Proscription of antidemocratic parties is a legal strategy whose consequences are unclear, and perhaps self-defeating or perverse. Two classes of mechanisms might operate in such situations, with opposing effects. The intent of proscription laws is to raise the cost of operating outside the liberal democratic framework; the expectation is that antidemocratic parties will moderate their positions and acquiesce in the system. The contrary possibility, however, is that the proscription itself will increase the violent tendencies of antidemocratic parties. One mechanism involves group polarization: if proscription laws force radicals to associate solely with other radicals, extremist individuals may push each other to become yet more extreme.[72] But even if individuals' views remain constant, there is also a noteworthy argument from selection effects: proscription laws may deter only the least radical individuals from joining antidemocratic parties, thus ensuring that proscribed parties are composed solely of individuals with the most radical dispositions.[73] In that case, proscription may reduce the membership of extremist parties, but increase the average radicalism of the remaining members, plausibly making the party a more serious threat to liberal democracy than it was initially.

If the latter set of effects dominates, proscription laws may exacerbate the problem they are intended to solve. A better strategy for law, in this scenario, would be to allow even openly antidemocratic parties to compete for political power in the hope of co-opting them through the political process itself. If no antidemocratic party can win an outright majority (or, in a first-past-the-post electoral system, an outright plurality), then the need to form alliances with democratic parties may force adoption of more moderate positions.[74] Comparative political history suggests that twentieth-century communist parties in Europe and Scandinavia were often co-opted, and moderated, by electoral alliances with social democrats and other nonrevolutionary parties of the left.

It is hard to say anything very general about such questions; the effects of the opposing mechanisms depend largely on local political institutions. It is clear, however, that incentive-based arguments cannot even identify the right questions, let alone answer them. Both the concern that official toleration for the intolerant may bring intolerant officials into power, and the idea that proscription laws radicalize opposition groups by excluding the least radical individuals, are selection arguments that focus on the composition of the pool of political actors, rather than the incentives of political actors already on the stage. Here, as elsewhere, selection analysis is a crucial analytic tool for identifying the dynamic effects of constitutional regimes; incentive arguments are too static to supply a complete analytic framework.

SELECTION AND SYSTEMIC CONSEQUENCES

The most general points I have tried to illustrate are that selection has feedback effects, and that selection analysis is a critical tool for examining the diachronic system effects of constitutional rules. Under what conditions will the indirect systemic consequences of selection prove most or least important? As a first approximation, selection analysis becomes more useful as we become more interested in the long-run effects of constitutional rules, as the pool of potential candidates for government office becomes more heterogeneous, and as constitutional rules affect the explicit or implicit compensation, or net costs and benefits, of officeholding. I will take up these ideas in turn.

Long-term versus short-term analysis. Constitutional analysis may legitimately concern itself with shorter or longer time-slices. In the short run, incentive-based analysis dominates, just because the time scale of the analysis deliberately assumes away the dynamic feedback effects of constitutional rules on the selection, over time, of the legislative, executive, and judicial officials themselves. But selection analysis dominates incentive analysis in the long run.

An example involves game-theoretic models of "self-enforcing constitutions,"[75] in which structures such as representative democracy and judicial review arise from compromises between risk-averse parties or groups who each prefer to lower the stakes of political conflict.[76] This is a strictly incentive-based approach; on this view, "the problem of constitutional stability is in large part one of incentives: do political officials have the appropriate incentives to honor the constitution?"[77] This analysis is important but also incomplete, because the focus on the incentives of political officials overlooks the feedback effects of constitutional structures on the identity of the very officials at issue. Quite plausibly the key strategy for creating a self-enforcing constitution is not, or not solely, to design appropriate incentives for whatever officials happen to hold power, but to choose self-stabilizing selection rules that bring to power officials who will tend to respect the constitutional rules previously laid down. No incentive-based analysis can adequately address that dimension of the constitutional designers' task.

Heterogeneous candidate pools. As we have seen, incentive analysis assumes that officials are motivationally homogeneous. On this view, constitutional rules must necessarily focus on providing the right incentives for current officeholders, because the alternative of attempting to pick well-motivated officials is simply not available; officials and potential officials are uniformly assumed to be self-interested. The most distinctive versions of selection analysis, by contrast, proceed on the assumption that potential officeholders are motivationally heterogeneous.[78] The candidate pool contains both good types and bad types, both well-motivated candidates and ill-motivated ones. Where types can be directly discerned, constitutional rules should attempt to do so; where they cannot be directly discerned, screening and sanctioning devices may indirectly accomplish the same end by creating differential incentives that encourage good types to sort themselves into official careers.

Effects on official compensation. Incentive analysis is most likely to go astray when constitutional rules affect the explicit or implicit compensation that officials derive from officeholding. That compensation may be pecuniary, as in the Ascertainment Clause of Article I and the Compensation Clauses of Articles II and III, but nonpecuniary compensation is important across a far broader range of constitutional rules. Most importantly, officials with altruistic or public-spirited motives may derive utility from posts that allow them to implement beneficial collective solutions, and may derive disutility from incentive-based schemes that assume all officeholders to be venal or ill-motivated. Incentive-based analyses that overlook the ex ante problem facing potential officeholders—the decision whether to seek or accept office in the first instance—will ignore the possibility that the incentives themselves may detract from the implicit compensation of well-motivated officials. In such cases incentive-based constitutional rules may discourage the well-motivated from seeking public office, and may thus exacerbate, rather than alleviate, the problem of self-interested official action.

Systemic feedback effects arising from selection are often uncertain. I have canvassed a number of more or less speculative examples to show the breadth of the domain in which selection analysis is potentially useful, but I have not claimed that selection analysis invariably yields determinate conclusions. But incentive analysis is also complex and often indeterminate, as the reams of conflicting incentive-based analysis demonstrate. Selection analysis provides no easy answers, but it is indispensable to a systemic perspective on the dynamics of constitutionalism.

CHAPTER 5

Constitutional Judging

The traditional subject of legal theory is judging, especially from the internal standpoint of the judge. So too the traditional subject of constitutional theory is constitutional judging, especially from the internal standpoint of the judge. Having examined constitutional structure throughout the preceding chapters, I turn now to a systemic view of constitutional judging—especially judging by justices of the U.S. Supreme Court. However, I will also consider decisions by other actors that bear more or less directly on judging, such as the appointment of judges by presidents and senators. The aim is to show that a systemic perspective on judging is analytically indispensable, even from the internal standpoint of any given judge, and yields questions and implications that traditional legal theory has overlooked.

I will begin with problems of division. In this setting, the division problem is that even if some particular approach to constitutional judging is best for all judges, it does not follow that it would be best for any given judge. In other words, any given judge cannot uncritically assume that it would be best for her to adopt the approach that would be best for all if adopted by all. Other judges may adopt a different approach, and if they do, then the nature of the best approach for the given judge may itself change, taking others' actions as nonideal constraints. It follows, I will suggest, that *strategic legalism*—a form of principled consequentialism—can be best for the judge concerned, under certain conditions. I apply these ideas to illuminate the problems faced by various approaches to judging and their adherents, including traditionalist Burkean judges in a non-Burkean world, deferential Thayerian judges in a non-Thayerian world, self-limiting minimalist judges in a world of maximalists, and historically minded originalist judges in a nonoriginalist world.

Throughout, I invoke these schools of theory in deliberately stylized form, and only for conceptual clarity. Actual judges are usually eclectic about legal methods and sources; most Burkean judges acknowledge grounds for overruling precedent, while most originalists will give some weight to precedent under some circumstances. However, because different judges inevitably attach different weights to available legal methods and sources, one can describe judges as more or less Burkean if they weigh precedent especially heavily, more or less originalist if they weigh the original understanding especially heavily, and so forth.

I then turn to problems of composition. In this setting, the composition problem is that even if some particular approach to constitutional judging would be best for any given judge, it does not follow that it would be best for all judges. To the contrary, methodological diversity will, under certain conditions, be a desirable property for the court or the judiciary as a whole. Where those conditions hold, the systemically minded judge would become a *legal chameleon* who changes her approach as the composition of the judiciary changes around her. Even if no judges are capable of being legal chameleons, a diverse portfolio of judges with different principled commitments can be attained by wise appointments to the bench.

PRINCIPLED CONSEQUENTIALISM

As the later discussion makes clear, I will assume that the "principled" judge is a consequentialist who chooses a theory of adjudication on the basis of its results. Not, however, on the basis of its policy results in particular cases, but either on the basis of its legal results in particular cases or on the basis of its long-run results for the legal system. The first is an act-consequentialist approach, the second a rule-consequentialist one. In either version, I do not believe the assumption is very restrictive; it subsumes even Ronald Dworkin, whose theory of adjudication—law as integrity, in which judges attempt to make law the best it can be along the dimensions of "fit" and "justification"[1]—is avowedly consequentialist.[2] And as we will see, even originalists have lately turned to arguments that justify originalist adjudication on essentially rule-consequentialist grounds.

Consequentialism need not entail welfarism, and this is another reason that the assumption is not very restrictive. It is perfectly possible for judges to adhere to a consequentialism of rights[3] or a consequentialism of legal entitlements, in which the judge attempts to ensure that legal entitlements (defined according to whatever independent theory the judge holds) are enforced to the maximum possible extent, regardless of the welfare effects of doing so. Conditional on consequentialism, the problems of system effects and the second best that I will discuss are entirely agnostic as among various first-order theories that define what counts as a correct legal outcome. Accordingly, I will consider arguments premised on a range of first-order theories, attempting to show that every such theory must confront systemic problems, and that such problems have a common structure. Although in any given context I will couch the discussion in terms of one or another first-order theory, that is merely for concreteness; the analysis goes through, with appropriate modifications, no matter how the first-order theory is specified.

DIVISION AND STRATEGIC LEGALISM

When traditional legal and constitutional theory addresses judging, it assumes that the key question is to find the best approach to judging. Once the theorist identifies an approach, the theorist typically goes on to argue that all judges should adopt that approach; and the theorist concludes, usually implicitly, that any given judge should adopt the approach. But that conclusion cannot logically be derived from the premise that all judges should adopt the approach. It is a fallacy of division to suppose that what would be best for all must necessarily be best for each.

Even if all judges should adopt a given theory, it does not follow that any one should, because others may not. The choices of other judges constrain the choices of any given judge, so each faces a strategic situation, the province of the theory of collective action and of game theory. From the standpoint of any given judge, choices by other judges create constraints that implicate the logic of *second-best adjudication*: what it is best to do given the constraints arising from others' choices may well differ from what it would be best to do if all other judges adhered to the same theory. (Here and throughout, "all" is not necessarily to be taken literally; I use it as shorthand for whatever critical mass of judges is necessary to produce the consequences posited by the relevant theory.)

In principle, this problem arises in two versions, one synchronic and one diachronic. The synchronic version involves interpretive theories that require some critical mass or threshold number of *current* judges to work as intended. The diachronic version involves action by *past* judges that is irreversible or costly to reverse. (I will use "irreversible" as shorthand for any past action whose reversal would require substantial costs.) In both versions, the disagreement of other present judges or the irreversible action of past judges function as constraints that trigger the logic of second-best adjudication for a current judge. The two problems often overlap or occur simultaneously, however, so I will treat both problems together in the setting of particular examples.

Democracy-forcing as a step good. Many interpretive approaches and tools are justified on the ground that they will elicit or force democratically desirable responses from other institutions, particularly legislatures; let us call this type of approach *democracy-forcing.* Proponents of textualism—the approach to interpretation that counsels the judge to follow the ordinary meaning of binding legal texts— sometimes assert that it increases the quality of legal drafting ex ante.[4] Likewise, a variety of quasi-constitutional interpretive principles and maxims, default rules, and canons of construction have been justified by reference to their effects on legislators and other democratic actors. By forcing legislators to speak clearly if they wish to override the relevant principles, the hope is to focus legislators' attention on the values the principles protect and to encourage democratic deliberation. Examples include the principle that statutes should be construed, where fairly possible, to avoid constitutional questions, and the principle that ambiguous criminal statutes should be construed in favor of defendants—the "rule of lenity."

A problem arises when, and to the extent that, democracy-forcing approaches require collective action by some threshold number or critical mass of judges, at a given time or over time, in order to achieve their effects. Where such thresholds exist, then even if it would be desirable for a critical mass of judges to engage in democracy-forcing interpretation, it does not follow that it is desirable for an *individual* judge to do so; that inference is a fallacy of division. Whether it is desirable for an individual judge to do so depends upon what other judges do—upon whether the judicial system can coordinate on the collective action needed to produce the democracy-forcing effects that the relevant interpretive principles are supposed to achieve.

When some critical mass is required for the interpretive principle to work, then democracy-forcing interpretation has the character of (what economists call) a step good: until the threshold needed for the efficacy of collective action is crossed, isolated judicial votes to engage in democracy-forcing interpretation make no marginal contribution to the good's provision and produce no marginal benefits. The requisite critical mass need not, of course, be 100 percent of the judges. On any given court, only a majority is required, although there must also be enough majorities on enough courts to achieve a critical mass at the level of the judicial system as a whole. The democracy-forcing effect will be undercut if different majorities on different courts take different views, and if shifting majorities on the Supreme Court prove unable, over time, to coordinate the interpretive system.

Indeed, the marginal benefit of democracy-forcing judicial votes may well be *negative* until the threshold of collective action is reached; unilateral acts of democracy-forcing by judicial panels or individual judges might be affirmatively harmful to litigants or the overall system, and thus perverse. For a schematic example, I will use textualism and one of its competitors, "intentionalism." The latter approach holds that legislators' intentions can at least sometimes trump the ordinary meaning of text, with intentions often found in the legislative history—the internal documents that legislators produce while enacting statutes. Suppose that (1) universal textualism by all judges is an equilibrium, in which legislative coalitions will place their instructions to the judges in the statutory text; (2) universal intentionalism is also an equilibrium, in which legislative coalitions will place their instructions in the legislative history; (3) the net social benefits of the textualist equilibrium are greater than those of the intentionalist equilibrium; and (4) the system is currently mired in the intentionalist equilibrium. An *isolated* textualist decision that eschews legislative history, on the theory that *universal* textualism would have beneficial democracy-forcing effects, would misread legislators' expectations in the case at hand without producing any countervailing social benefit, assuming that the isolated decision does not cause a critical mass of other judges to switch to textualism.

In some cases, the difference between step goods and ordinary public goods whose provision varies continuously with contributions can be finessed by seeing contributions to the step good as raising the ex ante probability that the good will be provided.[5] In the limit, the effect of judicial decisions might be perfectly divisible or marginal. For concreteness, consider the possible marginal democracy-forcing benefits of adding textualist judges to the judicial system. Increasing the number of textualist votes by 1 percent would then increase legislative incentives to draft responsibly by 1 percent.[6]

Yet this situation is only a theoretical possibility; it might or might not actually obtain, depending upon the distribution of the added votes, not just their number, and upon how the legislature responds to judicial decisions. In the previous example, where the judicial system is stuck in a suboptimal intentionalist equilibrium, adding textualist votes to the system will have *no* effect, not even a marginal one, if those votes are distributed across cases in the wrong way. In the limiting case, where textualist votes are only ever cast by dissenting judges, those votes are effectively wasted.

As to the second point, the legislative reaction to judicial decisions might well be lumpy, rather than perfectly divisible or marginal. This possibility can itself take two forms. In one version, the technology of drafting is inherently lumpy, so that legislators cannot make continuously variable marginal adjustments to respond to every 1 percent increase in judicial textualism. It may be, for example, that due to the inherent imprecision of language, the basic deal among the majority coalition can either be encoded in text or recorded in legislative history, but cannot be parceled out between text and legislative history with any arbitrarily desired degree of precision. In another version, the problem is not the technology of drafting but legislators' limited attention and cognitive capacities. Starting from a baseline case in which all judges are intentionalist, legislators might take no notice of textualism until the proportion of textualist judges or decisions reaches some critical mass and produces some highly salient outcomes.

Clearly, how legislatures respond to judicial decisions is an empirical question that cannot be decided in the abstract. Perhaps legislators accurately gauge and respond, at the margin, to a low probability that the judicial system will reach a textualist decision; perhaps they exaggerate and overreact to the low probability; perhaps they underestimate or ignore the low probability until enough textualists and textualist decisions are present to make the issue of judicial method salient and force it on the legislators' attention. In the last case, textualism justified on democracy-forcing grounds will be pointless, or even perversely harmful, unless and until some critical mass of other judges goes along.

Burkeans in a non-Burkean world. What is the role of precedent in judging? Here the division problem arises at two different levels. First, judges might not universally adhere to a theory of precedent that they universally share. Second, judges might have different theories of precedent altogether. At both levels, I will examine the dilemmas that arise for Burkean judges in a non-Burkean or partially Burkean world. Judges who think it desirable for the judiciary as a whole to attach a great deal of weight to precedent—what I will very loosely call Burkean judges[7]—might do best to adopt a different approach to precedent if many other judges do not share their Burkean views.

As to the first level, suppose that judges experience a cost from voting in accordance with precedent whenever the precedent dictates a first-order result with which the judge disagrees, that all judges share a particular theory of precedent, and that it would be socially beneficial for the judiciary as a whole to actually comply with and follow that theory. It does not follow that any individual judge should do so, because of the logic of collective action. The judges are in a multiplayer game, which can be interpreted in several different ways.

In one interpretation, the game is a multiplayer Prisoners' Dilemma.[8] In any given case, considered as a one-time interaction, each judge's dominant strategy is to defect from following precedent no matter what other judges do. Because the game is repeated, however, things are not so bleak; cooperation among the judges can be an equilibrium, depending upon how much the judges discount the future, whether cooperation can be clearly identified, and whether various strategies of reciprocation and punishment (such as "tit-for-tat") are feasible in the given environment. Here the threat of *retaliatory judicial activism* might sustain precedent-following as a cooperative equilibrium. Yet a breakdown of cooperation can also be an equilibrium, and if that occurs, it is not obvious why the Burkean judge should cooperate unilaterally. Doing so imposes individual costs for no social benefits.

In a different interpretation, the game of precedent-following is not a Prisoners' Dilemma but a game of coordination, such as an Assurance Game.[9] Each judge's first choice is to cooperate by sincerely following Burkean practices of respect for precedent, because universal cooperation will be best for all. However, no judge is assured of what the other judges will do, and no judge wants to be a chump who plays the cooperative move unilaterally while others defect. If coordination fails, the result may be a cadre of Burkean judges who, against their inclinations, show little regard for precedent. Suppose that Burkean judges, who afford great weight to precedent, respect the decisions of "activist" judges, here defined as judges who afford little weight to precedent; suppose also that activist judges do not respect the decisions of Burkean judges. Over time, legal change will systematically tend to come from activist rather than Burkean judges, and will tend to occur in large leaps rather than in incremental, epistemically humble steps. Anticipating this, even the Burkean judges may afford little weight to precedent, and all judges will appear activist.

Let us now turn to the second level, at which judges disagree about the best theory of precedent itself. Some judges believe that precedents should never be overruled; some that precedents may be overruled if and only if there is clear error; and some that both clear error and a special justification, such as an intervening change in legal or factual circumstances, is required. The situation may be interpreted as a mixed game of coordination and distribution—a Battle of the Sexes—in which each judge would prefer that the whole court or judiciary coordinate on some theory of precedent or other, yet each also wants the judiciary to coordinate on her preferred theory.[10] In such cases, it is possible that the group will be unable, over time, to coordinate on any stable regime, because players hold out for the regime they favor.[11]

The following sequence illustrates this possible instability, over time, in the theory of precedent. In Period 1, a given theory of precedent prevails in the legal system—say, a theory requiring special justification to overturn precedent, so that mere error is not enough. Call this the Burkean theory of precedent. In Period 2, a sufficient majority of the judges use a different, less demanding non-Burkean theory to overturn precedents decided during Period 1. We will stipulate that such precedents could not have been overturned according to the Period 1 Burkean theory. In Period 3, Burkean judges once again form a majority. According to their theory of precedent, may the Period 2 precedents be overruled? One answer is yes, because those precedents themselves rested on a mistaken theory of precedent. Another answer is no, because mere mistake is not a sufficient basis for overruling.

The Burkean judges face a dilemma: they must either apply their own theory of precedent retroactively, thereby increasing the instability of the legal system through overrulings of past nonconforming decisions, or else apply their own theory of precedent strictly prospectively, thereby confirming the validity of past decisions that support a different theory. Although the first best, for Burkeans, would occur if all judges had adopted the Burkean theory of precedent ab initio and consistently followed it over time, that possibility is ruled out by the disagreements of other judges, and Burkeans are constrained to choose between two distinctly second-best options. The dilemma is exemplified by the position of judges who believe that the post-1937 Roosevelt Court cavalierly discarded settled constitutional rules, and who must in turn decide whether to discard the settled constitutional rules generated by the Roosevelt Court. Another example is the position of judges who believe that the Warren Court cavalierly discarded constitutional rules of criminal procedure and due process, and who must decide whether to discard those precedents in turn.

Thayerians in a non-Thayerian world.[12] A Thayerian judge is a judge who upholds legislation against constitutional challenge whenever the legislation is premised on a reasonable understanding of the Constitution. Within this broad rubric, there are different ways of specifying Thayerism. Some Thayerian judges may hold that a reasonable reading of constitutional text is required; some may hold that a reasonable account of original understandings, or of precedent, is required. Some especially capacious Thayerians may hold that the legislation should be upheld so long as it can reasonably be justified in terms of *any* of the standard sources of constitutional law. These distinctions, however, are not material to the second-best problems facing Thayerians, which are the same however the approach is specified.

Consider the problems facing Thayerian judges in a largely non-Thayerian world. In particular, imagine a constitutional order whose history is much like our own. In this constitutional order, most judges have not been Thayerian most of the time, at least not for many decades, and at least not globally. Locally, there are pockets of constitutional law in which the Court defers to any reasonable congressional enactment—the judges call this "social and economic legislation"—and there have been brief periods in which a majority of the Court was globally Thayerian. However, Thayerism has little or no purchase in the domain of "individual rights" and a distinctly mixed record in the domain of "structural" problems such as federalism and the separation of powers.

In this world, it is hardly obvious that the judge who would be Thayerian if other current judges were Thayerian, and if past judges had been Thayerian, would want to be Thayerian in the circumstances she actually faces. Two problems are especially serious: the irreversible effects of non-Thayerian action by judges in the past, and the distorting effects of partial or local Thayerism in the present.

Irreversible effects. Thayerism is premised on a dynamic account of legislative capacities to interpret the Constitution in a responsible fashion. On this account, vigorous judicial review creates a "judicial overhang"[13] or moral hazard effect: anticipating that the judges will catch their constitutional mistakes, legislators will make more mistakes. This is, in effect, a systemic argument: it is a fallacy of composition to think that if one opinion on constitutionality (that of the enacting legislature) helps to safeguard the Constitution, then adding another opinion on constitutionality (that of the courts) will safeguard the

Constitution all the more. On the contrary, if the presence of the second institution induces more errors by the first and the second is an imperfect detector of the errors of the first, then adding an additional safeguard might increase the risk that the system will approve unconstitutional legislation.[14] Conversely, the argument runs, Thayerian judicial review will encourage legislators, who are aware that constitutional buck-passing is impossible, to be constitutionally responsible.

The problem is that if constitutional adjudication has been largely non-Thayerian for a long time, legislators may, according to the Thayerian theory itself, have been conditioned to constitutional irresponsibility. If so, a switch to Thayerism might produce the worst of all possible worlds: deferential judges upholding constitutionally irresponsible statutes. In the strongest form of this scenario, a constitutional culture and a set of legislative institutions have grown up that are systematically and permanently incapable of taking the Constitution seriously, and the courts lack the capacity to dispel that culture or reform those institutions. In a weaker form, a return to Thayerism would have beneficial dynamic effects in the long run, but the *interim* costs of legislatures' constitutional irresponsibility in the short run would be so great that they would dwarf the social gains from moving to Thayerism. Non-Thayerism might then amount to a sticky local maximum, analogous to the problem that arises when the transition costs of switching to an intrinsically superior technology are greater than the benefits of the switch.[15]

In either case, it may be true both that (1) Thayerism would have been best if followed consistently by all judges ab initio and also that (2) Thayerism would produce the worst possible state of affairs if introduced into a non-Thayerian world. From the standpoint of a Thayerian judge in such a non-Thayerian world, then, the second best might be non-Thayerism. In an environment in which past judges were Thayerian and other current judges are Thayerian, this judge would happily concur, but the judge will not advocate a switch to Thayerism in a second-best world.

Partial Thayerism. There is a synchronic version of the same problem, involving the choice among (1) global Thayerism across all areas of constitutional adjudication, (2) partial or local Thayerism applying to only some areas of constitutional adjudication, and (3) global non-Thayerism. For the Thayerian judge, (1) is clearly the top-ranked choice. Suppose, however, that the choices of other past and current judges place (1) off-limits. Whatever the nature of constitutional adjudication, it will not be globally Thayerian. What is the second best choice for the Thayerian judge? On the logic of the second best, it is not necessarily the case that (2) is better than (3), even though (3) has no Thayerism in it at all. The Thayerian alert to systemic effects might well prefer (3) to (2), assuming (1) is unavailable.

Suppose, for example, that the Thayerian judge believes that global Thayerism is best because it produces a maximum of overall welfare, taking into account the costs and benefits of all possible global interpretive approaches. As compared to global originalism, global textualism, and other approaches, the Thayerian believes that Thayerism produces the best sum of decision costs, error costs, and costs of legal uncertainty. Now let us stipulate that in some domain—perhaps "individual rights"—other judges are resolutely non-Thayerian. Thayerism only for domains other than individual rights will now produce additional systemic costs that can, in principle, tip the balance in favor of global non-Thayerism.

These systemic costs arise from the distortions created by differential standards of review in different areas of constitutional law. At the margin, legislators who incur net costs if their statutes are invalidated will have an incentive to pursue their policy goals by regulating "social and economic" matters, rather than through direct regulation of "individual rights," even if the latter course of action would be best overall. Moreover, there will be increased costs of litigation and legal uncertainty in cases where statutes can plausibly be described in either fashion. If these costs are sufficiently large, the Thayerian judge might think it better to give global heightened scrutiny to all statutes than to give deferential scrutiny only to some subset of statutes, even if universal deference would be best of all.

Minimalists in a maximalist world. Similar problems face the minimalist judge, who thinks it best for the court to issue narrow and shallow decisions—decisions that (1) do not decide a great deal and (2) rest on "incompletely theorized agreements"[16] among judges with different views. If other judges are not minimalist, then the minimalist judge may have to become a maximalist in self-defense. Even if the minimalist judge is motivated strictly by systemic considerations and cares only about contributing to a collective court that produces the best results overall, the same result can follow.

The basic rationales for global minimalism are that it minimizes the risks and costs of making large, irreversible errors, because the minimalist court takes only small and reversible steps in any given direction; that it leaves room for democratic or legislative responses to judicial decisions; and that it enables agreement on particulars among judges who disagree on fundamentals.[17] Suppose, however, that a majority of the court will issue wide and deep decisions, not narrow and shallow ones, and the court's minimalists are in the minority. In such a world, minimalism at the level of individual judges lacks the effects that are supposed to justify global minimalism by all judges. The court as a whole will take sides on fundamentals and will take large steps, creating risks of important and irreversible errors; the minimalist judge will not be able to stop it from doing so.

In such circumstances, the minimalist judge might do best to give up minimalism and instead attempt to ensure that the large steps the court will take are, at least, steps in the right direction, whatever that is.

The minimalist judge on a majority-maximalist court, therefore, faces a standard dilemma for reformers, who must choose between protesting the system from the outside and working for improvements from within. In the case of the minimalist judge, the choice is between dissenting in the hopes of influencing future judges to become minimalist and working to influence the direction in which the majority coalition goes, even if the steps the majority coalition takes and the rationales it advances are larger and more heavily theorized than the minimalist would prefer.

Originalists in a nonoriginalist world. In recent years, several theorists have attempted to give originalist constitutional adjudication a new justification in terms of consequences.[18] In this burgeoning body of work, the argument is that originalist adjudication has beneficial effects for the legal system as a whole. Usually, this argument takes a rule-consequentialist form rather than an act-consequentialist one: "Given a sufficiently good constitutional text, originalists maintain that better results will be reached overall if government officials— including judges—must stick to the original meaning rather than empowering them to trump that meaning with one that they prefer."[19]

Why do rule-consequentialist originalists believe that originalism, as opposed to other modes of adjudication, produces the greatest net benefit overall? Several answers are possible. First, originalism might minimize judicial discretion, and this might in turn reduce legal uncertainty or produce other systemic benefits. This seems unlikely, however, compared to other approaches. Thayerism, or even deciding cases by a coin flip, would both reduce judicial discretion more than would originalism, which requires the exercise of thick judgment about the import and weight of originalist sources.[20]

Second, originalism is sometimes justified on the consequentialist ground that it promotes democracy, but this too seems suspect. Originalism counsels that judges invalidate the current products of majoritarian lawmaking if the original understanding so requires, which in turn creates the notorious problem of the "dead hand." To be sure, democracy need not entail rule by contemporary majorities, but it requires theoretical epicycles to depict control of current majorities by long-dead generations as the summa of democracy.[21]

Given the infirmity of these answers, originalists have recently turned to a third argument: originalism produces good consequences because the original Constitution was a good one.[22] The original Constitution emerged from supermajoritarian procedures that tend, on average, to produce better constitutional law than do the majoritarian procedures used by current democratic legislatures. Following the original Constitution, where it conflicts with current democratic lawmaking, is thus beneficial on average.

Problems with originalism. I will suggest that this third argument rests on a fallacy of division. Even if it would be best, in the rule-consequentialist sense, for all judges to be originalist, it is not necessarily best for only some judges to be originalist in a partially nonoriginalist world. The consequentialist argument for originalism fails because most judges most of the time have not been originalist, with episodic exceptions, a fact that originalists explicitly lament.[23] Whatever the consequentialist credentials of originalism ab initio, introducing originalism into a largely nonoriginalist system founders on problems of the second best.

Because most judges have not been originalist, the current originalist judge lives in a world of constitutional law shaped, in large part, by nonoriginalist judges. *Universal first-best originalism* is unattainable; there are at least some nonoriginalist decisions of the past that are too costly to undo. In this second-best world, departures from the original understanding by nonoriginalist judges constrain what originalist judges can do today, and this means, according to the usual logic of the second best, that unless the originalist understanding of the Constitution is fulfilled in every case, the best consequences might well be obtained by departing from originalism on other margins as well. Given that a constitution is like the proverbial ship at sea that is constantly altered and rebuilt, implementing merely part of the original blueprint can have disastrous consequences, in light of intervening alterations to other parts of the structure.[24]

To pursue an example mentioned above, a view with strong support from some originalists is that the Constitution of 1789 prohibited delegations (or "excessive" delegations) to the president and also prohibited the legislative veto. If originalism had been consistently followed ab initio, constitutional law would contain both features. Given that nonoriginalist judges have allowed massive delegations, however, invalidating the legislative veto on originalist grounds removes one of the few remaining shackles on the executive and thus produces the worst possible outcome. The second best would be a form of nonoriginalist adjudication that permits a "translation" of original constitutional purposes,[25] or a compensating adjustment to the constitutional structure, by upholding the legislative veto.

Originalist responses. I will examine several lines of originalist response to this critique. In the most familiar response, stemming from Justice Antonin Scalia, originalists acknowledge that universal first-best originalism is unattainable, saying that they are "faint-hearted"[26] and will respect settled nonoriginalist precedents. The idea seems to be that precedent merely acts as a side-constraint on the outcomes that originalism would otherwise indicate, and leaves the originalist free to pursue those outcomes where precedent is not on point. This fallback view, however, is precisely what the general theory of second best makes problematic, at least if originalism is justified by reference to its consequences. The combination of the results that are untouchable with the originalist results that are still permissible may well have worse consequences than would a package containing *no* originalist results at all.

Justice Scalia's view accepts that there are some nonoriginalist decisions that are too costly to undo, although it underestimates the severity of the problem. Alternatively, consequentialist originalists might deny that there are any nonoriginalist decisions that are too costly to undo, in which case there would be no precedential constraints to trigger the general theory of second best. In one version of this view—which I am not sure anyone actually holds—originalist judges should simply reverse nonoriginalist precedents though the heavens fall. However, the resulting backlash would ensure that the only fall would be that of the judges who behaved so senselessly, and of the theory that drove them to do so. The final result would be, not universal first-best originalism, but a repudiation of originalism altogether—a consequence that originalists who justify originalism by reference to its consequences could hardly welcome.

In a more plausible version, originalism itself can build in scope for respecting precedents that supply reasonable "liquidating" constructions of provisions whose original meanings are intrinsically general or ambiguous, that have generated reliance by identifiable individuals, or that provide epistemic aid in determining original meaning.[27] In this version, the reason that there are no nonoriginalist decisions that are too costly to undo is not that every decision can be undone, but that any decision that is too costly to undo can be squared with originalism by fitting it into one of the categories of permissible precedent.[28]

I believe that this version of consequentialist originalism fails, however. I am not sure whether all of these categories are consistent with the consequentialist theory that is supposed to underwrite adherence to originalism in the first place, but even if they are, the problem is that they threaten to encompass either too little or too much. They encompass too little if they do not square originalism with major examples of irreversible nonoriginalist precedent, such as the decisions creating the administrative state, and too much if they allow any nonoriginalist precedents to be squared with the theory and thus draw originalism's fangs altogether.

As the second risk is self-explanatory, let me illustrate the first. It is an article of faith among originalists that *Myers v. United States*[29] correctly identified the original meaning of the Article II Vesting Clause and of the Take Care Clause, and thus held correctly that it is unconstitutional to make executive officials partially independent of the president by making them removable only for cause.[30] Let us stipulate for the sake of argument that this is true, and see what follows. Later decisions like *Humphrey's Executor v. United States*,[31] which unceremoniously discarded *Myers's* elaborate analysis,[32] do not fall into the category of "liquidating" precedent, because they overruled the earlier originalist precedent that did the liquidating, and do not even purport to supply an epistemically useful originalist construction of the relevant provisions. Assuming the independence of the independent agencies is a fixed feature of our institutional landscape, such cases cannot be squared with even a capacious version of originalism. They remain as irreversible nonoriginalist precedents that rule universal first-best originalism off the table, and thus trigger the problem of the second best.[33]

STRATEGIC LEGALISM

I am now in a position to generalize these examples, to state the basic idea of strategic legalism, and to say something about the conditions under which strategic legalism makes sense. Strategic legalism is not a descriptive claim—at the level of the Supreme Court, it turns out that the justices frequently ignore strategic considerations[34]—nor is it unconditionally normative. Rather, it is a conditional and prescriptive claim: even judges who decide strictly according to law must consider the possibility that the best attainable legal outcomes, by their own lights, will occur if they vote differently than they would if other judges agreed with their views. The behavior of other judges creates a non-ideal constraint on the behavior that is best for any given judge.

To define the issues more clearly, I will identify four ideal types of judges, who take different stances toward legal norms. The types are defined by their positions on two different axes: whether the judge is attitudinal or legalist, and whether the judge is strategic or nonstrategic.[35] Needless to say, real-world judges will not perfectly match any of the ideal types.

The first ideal type of judge is *attitudinal but nonstrategic*.[36] This judge votes her first-order policy preference in every case. If she is for gun control, then she votes to uphold gun control statutes, and vice versa if she opposes gun control. The attitudinal judge has no commitment to legalism at all, although for various reasons she may talk as though she does and may even believe that she does; it may be a case of self-deception or quasi-conscious bad faith rather than of deliberate deception of others.

The second ideal type of judge is both *attitudinal and strategic*.[37] This type of judge votes so as to maximize the satisfaction of her first-order preferences in light of the anticipated reactions of colleagues and of other institutions. Such judges are alert to the threat of reversals, legislative overrides, and other instruments of backlash. The consequence is that the attitudinal and strategic judge will always vote so as to move final outcomes as close as possible to her ideal policy point, but will sometimes vote in a manner that departs from her ideal policy point in a given case.

The third ideal type of judge is *legalist and nonstrategic*: she votes, in every case, in accordance with a legal theory about how constitutional or statutory provisions should be interpreted. The judge can be identified with an "ism"; she adheres to textualism, originalism, common-law constitutionalism, or some other theory. Again, real judges are usually eclectics rather than purists about theory, but as a matter of degree any given judge tends to weight some sources more heavily than others, and can thus be described as more or less an adherent of some ism or other. The points I will make thus come with a built-in qualification: they apply to the extent that the given judge is an adherent—perhaps only implicitly—of some theory or other.

The fourth ideal type of judge is a *strategic legalist*.[38] Both halves of the description are important. The strategic legalist judge cares only about ensuring the right legal results, as dictated by whatever legal theory she happens to hold. In this sense, she is not at all like the strategic but attitudinal judge, who takes account of the anticipated reactions of colleagues and other institutions strictly in order to maximize the satisfaction of her first-order policy preferences. Yet in contrast to the legalist nonstrategic judge, the strategic legalist does not simply vote in every given case in the way that her legal theory would dictate. Rather, she votes so as to move the law as close as possible to the outcomes her legal theory would dictate, in light of nonideal constraints, including what other judges and institutions will do. (I do not discuss other constraints that would arise even if there were only a single judge in the system. For example, a judge's own past pronouncements may constrain what she can say today, but this is not a systemic point—it does not derive from the collective character of appellate judging, in contrast to pronouncements from other judges past or present. It thus lies outside the scope of my theme, although it is compatible with my analysis.)

As the examples given earlier are intended to illustrate, the logic of division implies that under second-best conditions, strategic behavior by the legalist judge can produce better results than nonstrategic behavior, according to the judge's own legalist premises. The legalist nonstrategic judge, who ignores the behavior of others, implicitly votes in the way that would be best, according to her theory, if all other judges and other constitutional actors agreed. In a nonideal world, however, the approach that would be best if all other judges follow suit will not necessarily or even usually be best if other judges behave differently. It may in fact turn out to be best, under special conditions I will discuss below, but it cannot simply be *assumed* to be so.

By "best," I mean best according to the legalist judge's own lights, whatever they are. Even the judge who is committed to an account of what would make law the best it can be does not necessarily do best, as judged by that very account, by voting in every case in the way that would make law best if other judges were to agree. Because other judges will often not agree, the legalist judge may do best, according to her own theory, by voting differently than she would if all other judges were certain to vote likewise. What the legalist nonstrategic judge sorely needs, and lacks, is a nonideal theory of legal interpretation—a second-best approach to constitutional and statutory cases.

EVANGELISM, JUDICIAL CAPACITIES, AND SECOND-BEST NAÏVETÉ

The second-best approach that makes strategic legalism a live possibility is, by its nature, incapable of showing that strategic legalism is always superior under nonideal conditions. All it can show is that voting as would be best if other judges voted likewise need not be best under nonideal conditions. Are there particular nonideal conditions under which it would in fact be best for an individual judge to vote as she would in an ideal world?

I will explore two such conditions, respectively involving *evangelism*[39] and *limited judicial capacities*. In the first, the individual judge hopes that by ignoring second-best considerations and resolutely behaving as though the ideal world is present or close at hand, she will set a shining example that will eventually persuade other judges to convert to her preferred first-best theory. As such, evangelism can be understood as a sophisticated form of strategic naïveté: the evangelist's disregard for the consequences of her behavior in our fallen world so impresses the audience that it produces the very consequences for which the evangelist hopes. (Yet that effect cannot occur if the evangelist hopes to produce it, or at least if he is seen to have an eye on worldly rewards.)[40] Justice Thomas's opinions, which resolutely reject constitutional precedent in favor of a return to the revealed (original) meaning of the Constitution, often have this flavor.[41]

Of the many paradoxes that afflict this approach, I will limit myself to one that is relevant to my theme: evangelists rarely take into account the systemic effects that can arise if *other* judges display the same disposition. A bench of evangelists offering different gospels, far from effecting a mass conversion to any single evangelist's creed, might simply further entrench each other's beliefs, producing a vicious cycle of greater division and more intense evangelism. Moreover, in the eyes of the uncommitted audience, the very multiplicity of evangelists tends to cancel out the force of each. Decades of judicial proselytizing, in favor of various approaches, has not produced a mass conversion to any one approach, perhaps because the proselytizers offset one another.

I now turn to the second condition. Here the basic idea is that because of limits on judicial capacities, including epistemic capacities, judges might commit more and more serious mistakes—as determined by their own lights—by attempting to behave strategically than by woodenly behaving as they would in an ideal world. On this rule-consequentialist approach, judges would deliberately behave as though they are oblivious to problems of second best, because the uncertainty of the strategic environment creates intolerable epistemic burdens. Among the sources of uncertainty is the intrinsic indeterminacy of strategic interaction with other judges, given the chronic possibility of multiple equilibria in games with a coordination component.[42] Calculating that they have only uncertain prospects of advancing their legalist positions through strategic behavior in this kind of inherently indeterminate environment, judges decide that the most straightforward path is to ignore the strategic nature of the environment altogether.[43] Here too, judges would display a kind of second-order strategic naïveté that mimics the theoretical unsophistication of the idealist judge, who simply assumes that all others will see the world as he does.

Let me illustrate strategic naïveté—and its problems—by discussing the possibility of *second-best originalism*. I mean this in a different sense than the form of second-best originalism attributed to Justice Scalia in chapter 1. Justice Scalia's view of originalism as "the librarian who speaks too softly" works, if it works at all, only if followed by all judges ab initio, whereas the version of second-best originalism I am considering here attempts to address the problems created by nonoriginalist decisions in the past.

As we have seen, consequentialist originalists cannot argue for the benefits of originalism by imagining a world in which originalism triumphs ab initio and prevails consistently over time, for that world is not our own. It remains theoretically possible, however, that even in an irreversibly second-best world (from the originalist standpoint), naive originalism would produce greater net benefits than any interpretive approach that licenses judges to make or uphold compensating adjustments to the constitutional structure, such as the legislative veto. The argument would have to be that judges are ill-suited to identify valid compensating adjustments, so that the mistakes they make would have even more harmful consequences than would failure to adjust the constitutional rules to take account of systemic interaction between the originalist and nonoriginalist components of those rules.[44]

To make the argument concrete, imagine two possible worlds. In one, a regime with neither delegations nor the legislative veto is first best, a regime with both delegations and legislative vetoes is second best, and a regime with delegations and no legislative vetoes is third best. In this world, given delegations, judges should allow legislative vetoes as a compensating adjustment. In a different possible world, the second-ranked and third-ranked regimes are reversed, so that a regime with delegations and no legislative vetoes produces greater net benefits than a regime with both delegations and legislative vetoes. Judges in this latter world who erroneously believe they inhabit the former world will uphold the legislative veto, hoping to make a compensating adjustment that produces net benefits, but their action actually moves the system to the worst possible state. If this sort of mistake is sufficiently frequent and costly across the run of constitutional problems, then an interpretive approach that licenses judges to make compensating adjustments may actually be inferior overall to an approach that requires judges to behave *as though* they were naive first-best originalists, oblivious to the second-best problems.

In general, this sort of rule-consequentialist argument illustrates a large question of institutional competence: which constitutional actors, if any, should be licensed to make compensating adjustments, in light of the general theory of second best? Whatever its ultimate merits, on which I offer no judgment here, the rule-consequentialist argument for second-best originalism offers a very different type of justification than originalists typically offer. The strategically naive judge who decides to ignore second-best problems, on grounds of limited judicial competence and epistemic capacities, casts her vote on very different grounds than does the genuinely naive judge who is simply oblivious to the second-best problems, even if the two judges' observed behavior is identical.

Finally, let us be clear that problems of division affect the strategically naive judge no less than others. Even if it would be best for *all* judges to be rule-consequentialist originalists who are sufficiently sophisticated to mimic naive first-best originalists, it need not be best for any *given* judge to act that way, if other judges disagree. Suppose that (1) some judges are genuinely naive originalists; (2) other judges, although alert to the second-best problems with originalism, choose on rule-consequentialist grounds to behave as though they are naive originalists; (3) yet other judges attempt to practice enlightened second-best originalism or translation by making compensating adjustments to the constitutional structure. The overall result of the interaction between these three camps may be uncoordinated, incoherent, contested, or intermittent adjustments—plausibly the worst possible outcome for judges of all three types.

COMPOSITION AND THE LEGAL CHAMELEON

I now turn to the fallacy of composition, and its implications for adjudication. As with division, the conceptual error that underlies the composition fallacy is a mistake about generalization. In the division case, the error is to infer that if some interpretive approach is desirable when adopted by the whole court or judiciary, it must also be desirable when adopted by an individual judge. In the composition case, the error is to infer that if some interpretive approach is desirable when adopted by an individual judge, it must also be desirable when adopted by the whole court or judiciary.

That inference fails if methodological diversity is a desirable property of courts or of the whole judiciary. In economic terms, individual judges adopt approaches at the margin, but not every judge can be at the margin. An interpretive approach might be best when adopted by the additional or marginal judge, but not best when adopted by all judges. Indeed, under conditions in which diversity of interpretive method is a systemic good for the court or judiciary as a whole, the best judge might even be a kind of systemically minded legal chameleon, who would change her interpretive approach depending upon what mix of other judges is present on the court, until an equilibrium of optimal diversity is reached.

THE BENEFITS AND COSTS OF METHODOLOGICAL DIVERSITY

Although having a court composed of, for example, all textualists might be better or worse than having a court composed of all purposivists, it might be best of all to have a mixture of approaches. The basic intuition is that there are "diminishing returns to type":[45] on a multi-member court, the marginal benefits of having more of a given type of judge decline systematically, implying that a diversity of judicial types is best. Under what conditions might this intuition hold? What exactly are the benefits, and costs, of methodological diversity in a judicial group? I will confine the discussion to the benefits of methodological diversity within the highest court in the judicial hierarchy, such as the Supreme Court.

Epistemic accuracy. Let us begin with cases in which there is, by stipulation, a right answer to the legal question. (On some accounts, there is always a right answer, but I will remain agnostic about that claim.) This does not entail that the right answer is right *sub specie aeternitatis*, merely that the group shares at least some common aims and thus common fundamental preferences; their disagreements, if any, result from differing beliefs about the best means for promoting their common aims. As to the question of means, there can be a right answer for the group even if other groups with different aims might disagree.

As discussed in chapter 1, cognitive diversity contributes to the epistemic accuracy of groups. In a Jury Theorem framework, it has been shown, quite remarkably, that adding group members of worse-than-random accuracy can actually improve group performance, so long as the new members sufficiently reduce the correlation of errors across the group.[46] To the extent that diversity of interpretive method tracks or even produces cognitive diversity more generally, and thus reduces the correlation of errors across the group, then methodological diversity itself contributes to obtaining right answers.

But if there is disagreement about methods, what does it mean to say that the group is more likely to get the answers "correct"? By whose lights? Perhaps textualists believe the right answer just is the ordinary meaning of the text, while intentionalists believe the right answer just is the intention of the median legislator, and so forth. Then different judges will be asking different questions, in which case the logic of epistemic aggregation cannot apply.

Although doubtless true in some cases, this point overlooks a range of important cases in which methodological disagreement and first-order disagreement about right answers are fully compatible with meta-agreement on what would *count* as the right answer. In many cases, methodological disagreement really is about method—about what sources and tools judges should use to pursue their common goals. An important subspecies of textualist judge, for example, is the intentionalist who happens to think that the enacted text is the best or even exclusive evidence of intention. Here, both the intentionalist-qua-textualist and the all-out intentionalist are asking the same ultimate question—what are the legislators' intentions?—although they look to different sources to answer it.

Preventing polarization. Like-minded judges share empirical assumptions and normative commitments that may be exaggerated by the presence of other like-minded judges.[47] As to issues that range along a single dimension (say, whether to give more or less weight to the rule of lenity), deliberating groups of like-minded judges may polarize in the direction of the predeliberation mean, and thus go to extremes.[48] Where the predeliberation mean is bimodal, so that opposing views are each well-represented, this effect is suppressed.

Whether preventing polarization is a benefit depends upon whether going to extremes is generally bad, a point I will take up next. If it is bad, or in cases where it is bad, this point does useful work; it supplies psychological microfoundations for the idea that methodologically diverse groups will tend to avoid large mistakes in any direction.

Moderation of competing approaches. Diversity of interpretive approaches, methods, and perspectives will tend to moderate judicial approaches and outcomes.[49] Suppose, for example, that interpretive formalism is not an on-off switch, but a continuum. We can well imagine that a group of textualist judges might always interpret statutes and constitutional provisions in a highly literalistic fashion; a group of purposivist judges might always interpret statutes and constitutional provisions in an extremely plastic, policy-sensitive fashion; and a group with diverse approaches might often follow the apparent meaning of legal texts but might occasionally tailor text to reasonable conceptions of original intentions or purposes.

Is this moderation good? Theorists strongly committed to one approach or the other might say that moderation is neither here nor there. If a moderate court gets the right outcome, as judged by the theorists' preferred approach, then moderation is good; otherwise it is not. Polarizing in the right direction is good; in the wrong direction, bad. But this point, unimpeachable from within the partisan perspective of any particular interpretive theory, is not helpful from the systemic standpoint. From that standpoint, the problem is how the overall court or judiciary should be arranged, given that many different camps of interpretive theorists each claims that *its* preferred approach is uniquely correct, and given that this disagreement over the correct interpretive theory seems intractable, at least for the foreseeable future. Under these circumstances, moderation has much to recommend it. The systemically minded judge—or, I shall add later, the systemically minded appointer of judges—who is uncertain which of the possible approaches is best might be wise to hedge the risks of wholesale adoption of one approach and wholesale rejection of its competitors. A methodologically diverse judiciary is, plausibly, the best way to minimize the risk that any particular approach will have bad consequences for the interpretive system.

In some cases, it is possible that moderation might actually increase the variance of outcomes. A bench composed solely of strict textualists, or of unsophisticated purposivists, might produce more predictable (even if more extreme) decisions than a bench featuring a mixture of interpretive approaches, just as a panel of extreme left-wing (or right-wing) judges might produce more predictable decisions than a mixed panel. Perhaps this is so, but perhaps it is not. For one thing, a bench of (say) all textualists might produce a set of decisions with equal variance, but now centered around a different, more extreme mean. Under genuine uncertainty about the direction and magnitude of effects of this sort, methodological diversity is the safest default position for the interpretive system.

Legitimation for multiple audiences. The audience for judicial decisions extends far beyond the litigants, or even other lawmaking institutions; it encompasses informed elites in the legal profession, the legal academy and universities generally, and the public. Different sectors of this audience have different convictions, often firmly held, about the proper approach to constitutional and statutory interpretation. The rulings of a methodologically diverse court might appeal to a broader segment of this audience than the rulings of a methodologically homogenous one. An originalist court might please originalists while dismaying nonoriginalists; a diverse court might produce rulings that create a greater overall level of satisfaction, and enjoy wider acceptance.

To make these suggestions more concrete, we may consider two perennial topics in American legal theory.

Formalism and functionalism in separation-of-powers law. The constitutional law bearing on separation of powers is famously riven by opposing methodological camps: so-called formalists and functionalists. Formalists argue for attention to text and original understanding, for rule-bound adjudication, and for clear lines of demarcation between the branches of the federal government,[50] except insofar as the branches have explicit constitutional authority to participate in each other's activities; the president's veto power is an example. Functionalists argue for flexible adaptation of the separation of powers to the exigencies of modern government, for standard-based or balancing approaches to separation-of-powers adjudication, and for participation by each branch in the decision-making processes of other branches.[51] On this view, the separation of powers merely prohibits one branch from appropriating or intruding upon the "essential functions"[52] of other branches.

Plausibly, a Supreme Court composed of both separation-of-powers formalists and functionalists would do better than a bench composed solely of committed adherents of one or the other approach. That answer will seem incoherent to partisans of either view. After all, each side will say—agreeing on this although nothing else—whether the Court can be said to do well in any particular case depends on whether it has adopted the correct approach to separation-of-powers law.

From the systemic standpoint, however, diversity hedges the risks of large mistakes in either direction. A Court staffed solely by functionalists such as Justices Rehnquist and White would systematically undervalue the virtues of a rule-like approach to separation-of-powers adjudication: stability, predictability, and fidelity to text and original constitutional design. A bench of this sort might approve ill-considered improvisations, hasty institutional arrangements that tamper with the Constitution's deep structure. In hindsight *Morrison v. Olson*[53] looks like a case of just this sort; the independent counsel law was, on this view, a harmful solution to a nonexistent problem.

On the other hand, the extremes of formalism also look unattractive; a bench composed solely of separation-of-powers formalists might choke off valuable structural reform, producing excessive rigidity in the lawmaking system. Consider the line-item veto decision, *Clinton v. City of New York*,[54] which uses strained formalist arguments to invalidate a bipartisan innovation that has been widely adopted in the states, and that is precious hard to distinguish from ordinary delegations of impoundment authority to the president.[55] Indeed *Clinton v. City of New York* is formalist in another, pejorative sense as well: the opinion conceals the majority's real concern, a nondelegation concern about transfers of excessively open-ended authority to the president, behind a dogmatic reading of the relevant constitutional texts.[56]

These examples suggest that a well-functioning approach to the separation of powers would minimize the sum of two types of errors: harmful decisions by political actors to tamper with constitutional structure for short-term advantage or poorly deliberated ends, on the one hand, and judicial rejection of valuable institutional innovations, on the other. Formalist judges are especially alert to the first type of mistake, functionalist judges to the second. A bench composed of both formalists and functionalists might detect enough of both errors to minimize their sum, relative to a uniform bench of either stripe.

Under imaginable assumptions, this possibility would not hold. If, for example, the Court is composed of five formalists and four functionalists, and the formalists always unite to invalidate constitutional innovations by a five-to-four vote, and if invalidation is an all-or-nothing proposition, then the collective outcome will be no different from that of a uniformly formalist Court. However, the assumptions behind this story are shaky. First, "formalism" and "functionalism" lie on a continuum,[57] so the marginal formalist (or functionalist) will likely be a methodological moderate who will occasionally swing to the other camp. Second, invalidation is not all-or-nothing, but can be of greater or lesser scope. The possibility of partial invalidation allows for moderate outcomes. Finally, if at least one justice is a legal chameleon and occupies a swing position on this dimension, then the chameleon can prevent either faction from dominating the decision making, ensuring that outcomes at the aggregate level of the whole Court will reflect methodological diversity.

In general, the details might be specified in several different ways, and outcomes at the level of the Court will be sensitive to the precise specification. But it is quite possible to think that a bench composed of justices with diverse views about separation-of-powers law would produce better structural constitutional law than a Court with uniform views in either direction. This claim is, however, plausible only for the judge who takes a systemic standpoint; from the standpoint of methodological partisans, it is incoherent.

Interpreting statutes to avoid absurd results. Consider also the question whether and when judges ought to interpret statutes to avoid absurd results. Intentionalists and purposivists are particularly alert to cases in which statutory text is overinclusive or (more rarely) underinclusive with respect to plausible conceptions of legislators' intentions or purposes. These interpreters propose that courts should have wide discretion to mold a statute to fit its underlying objectives and to avoid the bizarre or unjust consequences of literalism. Formalists and textualists, on the other hand, are alert to detect cases in which the judicial interpretation to avoid absurd results creates rather than avoids mistakes.[58] Formalists stumble over examples such as the Arkansas statute that inadvertently repealed the state's entire code of laws;[59] functionalists stumble over examples like the *Holy Trinity* case,[60] in which the Supreme Court invoked the absurd-results canon to exempt an English minister from a statute that prohibited contracting with an alien to perform labor or service of any kind in the United States.[61] A bench composed of both formalists and functionalists might do the best job of detecting and preventing both sorts of mistakes, thus minimizing their sum; a bench staffed solely by one camp or the other might do worse overall.

In a first-best world, the examples would show not that courts should be composed of methodologically diverse judges, but just that courts should avoid mistakes at either extreme. A court composed of a single judge—the limiting case of nondiversity—might, on this view, get all the cases right if the judge is sufficiently skilled at avoiding the mistakes that arise from either erroneous formalism or erroneous functionalism. The problem is that no actual judges, in the nonideal world of the judicial system, are capable of infallibly striking the optimum. Methodological diversity across a number of judges harnesses the partial and fallible commitments, expertise, and prejudices of different types of judges, alert to different types of mistakes to which interpretation is prone, and enlists them to produce the best overall results for the system as a whole.

SYSTEMIC JUDGING AND LEGAL THEORY

It is time to take stock of the systemic perspective on judging, and its implications for legal theory and legal institutions. What makes a good judge? How should the good judge interpret statutes and the Constitution? These are standard questions of legal theory, but as stated they are ill-defined; no answer can be given. What makes a good judge, and what the good judge would do, depends upon what *other* judges there are and what those other judges do. The qualities that it is desirable for judges to have, and the actions it is desirable for them to take, depend on the judicial and institutional environment in which they find themselves.

There are thus two distinct objections to Ronald Dworkin's mythical judge, Hercules.[62] The first is that Hercules has superhuman epistemic capacities, whereas real appellate judges have epistemic limits. That point is familiar, yet there is a second and equally important objection that only a systemic perspective can uncover: Hercules sits alone, whereas real appellate judges sit collegially. The second objection implies that what it is best for the judge to do is not a question that can be answered in isolation. Even a superhuman Hercules must operate in an environment where the behavior of other judges, not to mention other institutions, may affect what would otherwise be his best course of action.

To be sure, as I have tried to show in earlier chapters, the multi-member character of the appellate court may, under certain conditions, magnify the epistemic competence of its members, by virtue of the Jury Theorem. In that case, the second objection would itself provide a partial cure for the first. Furthermore, the judges may calculate that the cognitive costs of strategic legalism are too high, resulting in a sophisticated second-best naïveté that causes them to mimic the behavior of a judge, like Hercules, who ignores what other judges do. In that case, the first objection would itself provide a partial cure for the second. Needless to say, however, these possibilities require an entirely different type of analysis than Dworkin provides; his resolutely nonsystemic framework makes the questions themselves invisible.

Another implication of the systemic perspective is that where group-level diversity is desirable, the systemically minded judge will be a legal chameleon, who changes her colors as the environment changes. The legal chameleon acts so as to diversify the court on which she sits by adopting whatever interpretive method is underrepresented at the margin. Rather than copying her environment in order to camouflage herself, she will adjust so as to contradict the dominant tendency in her environment, reducing the risk of groupthink. The legal chameleon, then, might more accurately be called a counter-chameleon. She is a contrarian, but only insofar as contrarianism is beneficial for the group.

The legal chameleon has a measure of critical distance even from her own legal theory, whatever that is. She appreciates that the partisans of this or that interpretive theory may all do best if all are present within the court or judiciary but none dominate. This perspective seems incomprehensible to the partisans of any given theory or approach, who see the chameleon as having only derivative and tactical commitments rather than unconditional ones, and who do not think they can possibly be made better off by the presence of judges who deviate from (what they take to be) the "true" approach to understanding the Constitution. From the chameleon's standpoint, however, awareness of the limits of one's own knowledge suggests that the group should hedge the risk that any particular theory is erroneous. The best way to do so is to have an overall group of judges with diverse approaches.

One might think that not all judges can be legal chameleons; perhaps the property cannot fully generalize. If the legal chameleon adjusts her behavior in light of what other judges do, how can it be possible for all judges to do so simultaneously? On closer inspection, however, the difficulty is illusory. In principle, a full bench of legal chameleons could engage in a process of mutual adjustment, coordinating on an equilibrium that optimizes the methodological diversity of the court as a whole. The bench of chameleons would spread out across the methodological space, with some behaving as textualists, some as intentionalists or originalists, some as Burkeans, and so forth.

This scenario is patently fantastic, and it points to a real problem with the legal chameleon: some judges will find it too psychologically demanding to be so relentlessly flexible and systemically minded. For those judges, interpretive approaches are deeply held jurisprudential commitments, which cannot be taken off or put on like clothing. We ought not expect or demand, for example, that a judge whose prior beliefs or commitments are formalist or textualist should try to adopt a functionalist or intentionalist approach in order to diversify the court on which the judge sits. In reality, although some judges may be legal chameleons, many will not.

Happily, however, not all judges need to be. The legal chameleon supplies systemic benefits at the margin, by diversifying a court that would otherwise be dominated by a single perspective. Indeed, under certain conditions, the legal chameleon can wield outsized influence even if most or all other members of the court are staunch methodological partisans. If the partisans are split in opposing directions, the chameleon can supply decisive votes and thus determine the direction of the court as a whole—the miracle of judicial aggregation discussed in chapter 2.

Furthermore, because the benefits of methodological diversity are systemic rather than individualized, they can also be promoted at the systemic level. To the extent that methodological diversity is desirable, presidents ought to appoint nominees who are true believers in whichever approach will diversify, at the margin, the courts to which they are appointed. And under the same conditions, senators have a systemic obligation to cast confirmation votes with the benefits of methodological diversity in mind, rather than simply attempting to stock courts with a uniform cast of like-minded interpreters. Where this occurs, a diverse portfolio of methodological partisans will mimic, in second-best fashion, the results that a full bench of legal chameleons would produce.

JUDICIAL HOMOGENEITY AS A SECOND BEST?

A second-best approach to legal interpretation and adjudication cannot show that the legal chameleon's approach is always superior, just that its superiority is always possible. Above, I have tried to state conditions under which that possibility will materialize. Under what conditions might homogeneity of interpretive approaches among the judiciary nonetheless be best? In the spirit of the second-best model of judicial bias counteracting legislative bias, discussed in chapter 2, another possibility is that methodological homogeneity among the judges might be an indispensable counterweight to homogeneity among the nonjudicial branches.

Suppose that presidents and (a critical mass of) senators coordinate on a particular approach to constitutional interpretation, which they fervently believe to be correct. Then methodological homogeneity among the judiciary might be necessary to create a diversity of interpretive approaches in the system overall, although that diversity would hold across institutions rather than within the judiciary itself. For concreteness, suppose that presidents and senators uniformly favor originalist approaches to constitutional interpretation. Then the benefits of methodological diversity can be attained at the level of the overall lawmaking system only if the judiciary itself adopts a homogeneously nonoriginalist approach, one that is negatively correlated with the approach favored by nonjudicial officials. If the judges are already originalists, then—in this scenario—a bloc of nonoriginalists should be appointed.

I mention this possibility only because its systemic structure is analytically important. In the real world, even nonjudicial officials who take constitutional questions seriously do not typically coordinate on a particular approach to constitutional interpretation, for the simple reason that their major commitments and agendas, however public-spirited they may or may not be, are selected on grounds that are largely random with respect to the technical modalities of constitutional interpretation. In a world of eclectic and diverse views and commitments among nonjudicial officials, it is plausibly best for the judiciary to be methodologically diverse as well.

CONSTITUTIONAL JUDGING IN SYSTEMIC PERSPECTIVE

Chapter 2 examined judging from the external standpoint—of constitutional designers, or of analysts of the judicial system. This chapter offers a systemic analysis from the internal standpoint of relevant officials—principally judges, but also the officials who appoint judges. I hope to have shown that the systemic perspective redefines the questions, even where it does not, by itself, entail particular answers. From the standpoint of individual judges, the systemic perspective shows that standard theories of judging fall into conceptual mistakes by overlooking system effects, that judging is a profoundly collective enterprise, and that the judge should not naively adopt an interpretive approach by imagining herself in splendid isolation. (Derivatively, legal theorists who wish to offer judges advice from the internal point of view should not imagine the judge in splendid isolation either; I will return to this theme in the conclusion to the whole book.) Although a judge who appreciates the systemic character of judging may decide, for those very same systemic reasons, to behave as though she judges in isolation, that itself is an approach profoundly different than the naïveté of the judge who does not understand the systemic character of judging at all. From the standpoint of officials who appoint judges, the systemic perspective underscores the benefits of appointing a methodologically diverse portfolio of judges. In either case, the official who thinks systemically will approach matters very differently than does an official who is oblivious to system effects, even if the ultimate conclusions happen to be the same in particular cases.

Conclusion: Two Degrees of Aggregation

Problems of aggregation are not just central to constitutional theory; they are its very flesh and blood. Constitutional theorists often hive off aggregation problems to a few remarks about Arrow's Theorem, which rests on highly fragile assumptions and in any event merely embodies one particular approach within a particular branch of the theory of social choice. Yet in all constitutional orders, aggregation problems are ubiquitous and structural. All institutions are aggregates of interacting members,[1] and a constitutional order is itself an aggregate of interacting institutions. Between the individual action of judges, officials, and citizens, on the one hand, and the overall constitutional order on the other, there lie not one but two degrees of aggregation.

The problem for the constitutional theorist is that there are tricky relationships between aggregates and their members, between systems and their components. When these relationships are misunderstood, fallacies of division and of composition result; and in two-level systems, the pitfalls are not merely doubled, but multiply exponentially. My central claim, then, is that the systemic perspective is an indispensable analytic tool, especially in constitutional theory. Constitutionalism is a system of systems that arises from the interaction of individuals within institutions and the interaction of institutions within an overall constitutional order. Although under some conditions actors within systems may do best to ignore system effects, under other conditions actors will do best by taking into account that what is best for all may not be best for each, and that what is best for each may not be best for all. Legal analysts, for their part, cannot make sense of constitutionalism without understanding it in systemic terms.

Why have constitutional and legal theory largely ignored the systemic perspective? It is not that theorists have made no systemic arguments, at either of the two levels of aggregation; throughout, we have seen such arguments offered in local contexts, and with respect to particular problems. Yet the puzzle is that the theoretical structure of those arguments and the systemic analysis on which they rest has not been identified and considered as such.

Some possible answers are economic, historical, and jurisprudential. In economic terms, the costs of production are in part determined by the cost of the inputs to production, in scholarship as in other activities. Only recently have legal theorists had low-cost access to excellent theoretical accounts of aggregation problems in systems and the dynamics of feedback in systems.[2] With the cost of theoretical inputs reduced, it is now possible to arbitrage the framework of systems theory, and its relevant results, to produce an improved theory of constitutional institutions—one of my major aims here.

In historical terms, legal theory until recent decades has been closely tied to the legal profession as opposed to the university and its disciplines. The legal profession tends to take a nonsystemic, piece-meal approach to legal problems, focusing on particular cases and controversies—the legal issues of the day, great or small. Legal theorists who are oriented toward the profession tend to follow suit. But as academic theorists of law increasingly orient themselves to the social sciences and other university disciplines rather than the profession, they tend to take the aggregative perspective of economics, sociology, and (certain sectors of) political science, yielding the many localized and implicitly systemic results and arguments that I have tried to draw together in the preceding chapters.

Jurisprudentially, constitutional and legal theory have often been tied to the perspective of the individual judge. Jurisprudence per se—the analytic philosophy of law—aspires to offer a wider, external standpoint on the legal system, yet this body of theory is hampered by its intrinsic limitations, especially its quixotic attempt to identify essential or necessary or universal criteria for counting a system as a legal system, rather than treating legality as a "cluster concept" loosely generalized from a series of family resemblances.[3] Jurisprudence in the broader sense of legal theory obsessively adopts the internal stand-point of adjudication, explicitly or implicitly asking how "the judge"—and the legal theorist so often imagines himself as that judge—should decide particular cases. Ronald Dworkin's Judge Hercules is only the most famous example of this tendency;[4] even today, the bulk of constitutional theory takes the form of shadow opinion-writing in which the theorist asks what the ideal opinion in the case would say.

This perspective has its uses, but suffers from an inherent short-coming, which is that it abstracts away from the inherently collegial and therefore aggregative enterprise of judging on appellate courts.[5] In almost any modern legal system, the higher reaches of the judicial hierarchy are occupied by multimember judicial bodies who interact with multimember legislatures and a multiplicity of other institutions.

The implication is that between the individual judge and the outputs of the constitutional order two levels of aggregation intervene: from judges to the court or judiciary as a whole, and from the judiciary to the interacting system of lawmaking institutions. The topic of constitutional adjudication, then, is inherently systemic, and the traditional focus on "the judge" is patently inadequate.

This point holds from the internal standpoint of any given judge as well as from the external standpoint of the legal analyst. As I have tried to show in chapter 5, any given judge can make sense of her own individual task only by asking what other judges and other officials will do, by understanding that what is best for all may not be best for each, and that what is best for each may not be best for all. In this regard, most of the extant theory of constitutional adjudication is intrinsically ill-suited to the properties of the subject at hand. Consequently, I hope to have identified a more suitable set of questions, and to have shown why those questions should dominate the intellectual agenda of constitutional theory.

ACKNOWLEDGMENTS

I would like to thank many friends and colleagues for encouraging me to develop and bring together these ideas. Richard Fallon, Jacob Gersen, Jack Goldsmith, Don Herzog, Daryl Levinson, Jacob Levy, John Manning, Frank Michelman, Martha Minow, Eric Posner, Fred Schauer, Matthew Stephenson, Cass Sunstein, and Mark Tushnet provided invaluable comments on various parts of the material, and I also benefited from the comments of two anonymous reviewers for Oxford University Press. Janet Kim, Colleen Roh, and Sergei Zaslavsky provided excellent research assistance, Ellen Keng kept the system running with unfailing good cheer and competence, and David McBride and his colleagues at OUP were helpful and encouraging throughout. Most important of all, special thanks go to my family—Yun Soo, Emily, Spencer, and Blake—for their constant love and support.

I have been worrying at the topic of this book for several years now, approaching it from different angles. The book attempts to distill, summarize, integrate, and restate the conclusions of this process. Thus parts of the book have been adapted, with heavy modifications and rethinking, from several published articles, listed below. I thank the editors of the relevant journals and presses for permission to incorporate the material.

The Invisible Hand in Legal and Political Theory, 96 Virginia Law Review 1417 (2010).

Divide and Conquer, 2 Journal of Legal Analysis 417 (2010) (with Eric A. Posner and Kathryn E. Spier).

Foreword: System Effects and the Constitution, 123 Harvard Law Review 4 (2009).

Constitutional Amendments and the Constitutional Common Law, in THE LEAST EXAMINED BRANCH: THE ROLE OF LEGISLATURES IN THE CONSTITUTIONAL STATE 229–71 (Richard W. Bauman & Tsvi Kahana eds., Cambridge University Press 2006) (reprinted with permission).

Second-Best Democracy, 1 Harvard Law & Policy Review Online (2006), http://www.hlpronline.com/2006/11/vermeule_01.html.

The Judiciary Is a They, Not an It: Interpretive Theory and the Fallacy of Division, 14 Journal of Contemporary Legal Issues 549 (2005).

Selection Effects in Constitutional Law, 91 Virginia Law Review 953 (2005).

NOTES

INTRODUCTION

1. For accessible general introductions to systems theory and related ideas, see Scott E. Page, DIVERSITY AND COMPLEXITY (2011); Melanie Mitchell, COMPLEXITY: A GUIDED TOUR (2009); Donella H. Meadows, THINKING IN SYSTEMS: A PRIMER (2008); Scott E. Page & John H. Miller, COMPLEX ADAPTIVE SYSTEMS: AN INTRODUCTION TO COMPUTATIONAL MODELS OF SOCIAL LIFE (2007).
2. For general treatments, see Robert Jervis, SYSTEM EFFECTS: COMPLEXITY IN POLITICAL AND SOCIAL LIFE (1997); David Easton, A SYSTEMS ANALYSIS OF POLITICAL LIFE (1965).
3. For illuminating applications of systems theory to the problems of federalism, see Jenna Bednar, THE ROBUST FEDERATION (2009); and to administrative law, see Donald T. Hornstein, *Complexity Theory, Adaptation and Administrative Law*, 54 DUKE L.J. 913 (2005) and sources cited therein. The German sociologist Niklas Luhmann advanced a "systems theory" that he applied to law as well as other domains, but the theory does not have much to do with systems theory as understood in the social sciences, is notoriously obscure, and is difficult to cash out in an analytically precise or pragmatically relevant fashion. For an introduction to the theory and its difficulties, see Alexander Viskovatoff, *Foundations of Niklas Luhmann's Theory of Social Systems*, 29 PHILOSOPHY OF THE SOCIAL SCIENCES 481 (1999).
4. *See* Page & Miller, *supra* note 1, at 3 ("At the most basic level, the field of complex systems challenges the notion that by perfectly understanding

the behavior of each component part of a system, we will then understand the system as a whole").

5. See Christian List and Philip Pettit, GROUP AGENCY: THE POSSIBILITY, DESIGN, AND STATUS OF CORPORATE AGENTS 65–66 (2011).

6. This approach is consistent with the approach to group agency taken in List & Pettit, *supra* note 5. List and Pettit defend a "realist" view in which groups can have genuinely autonomous agency not reducible to the agency of their members, yet the ascription of agency to groups is consistent with methodological individualism; there is no mysterious group mind in the picture. See id. at 2–11. A semantic issue is that List and Pettit sometimes use the label "emergentist approach" to denote an approach that pictures "group agency as the product of [a] mysterious, organicist force." Id. at 9. The notion of "emergent properties" of groups, as I will use it, is just a more vivid synonym for "supervening properties" and does not require positing such a mysterious force. List and Pettit's theory is built around the possibility of group-level properties not reducible to the properties of individual group members, see id. at 8, 74–78, and that is all that the notion of emergent properties implies in the chapters that follow.

CHAPTER 1

1. This definition is adapted, with major modifications, from Robert Jervis, SYSTEM EFFECTS: COMPLEXITY IN POLITICAL AND SOCIAL LIFE 6 (1997).

2. *See* Marquis de Condorcet, *Essay on the Application of Mathematics to the Theory of Decision-Making, in* CONDORCET: SELECTED WRITINGS 33, 52–55 (Keith Michael Baker ed., 1976).

3. *See* Lewis A. Kornhauser & Lawrence G. Sager, *The One and the Many: Adjudication in Collegial Courts,* 81 CAL. L. REV. 1, 10–12 (1993).

4. *See generally* Anatol Rapoport and Albert M. Chammah, PRISONER'S DILEMMA: A STUDY IN CONFLICT AND COOPERATION (1965).

5. For formal renditions of these fallacies, with social science applications, see Jon Elster, LOGIC AND SOCIETY: CONTRADICTIONS AND POSSIBLE WORLDS 97–106 (1978); for economic applications, see Paul Samuelson, ECONOMICS: AN INTRODUCTORY ANALYSIS 8–9 (1 st ed. 1948). Philosophers of logic have identified several subcases, in which the fallacies can rest on either semantic, conceptual, or causal mistakes. See, e.g., *id.* at 98–103; William L. Rowe, *The Fallacy of Composition,* 71 MIND 87, 89–91

(1962). For the most part, my examples fall into the latter two categories; in any event, the philosophical refinements are not material for my purposes.

6. Paraphrasing Adam Ferguson, AN ESSAY ON THE HISTORY OF CIVIL SOCIETY 119 (Fania Oz-Salzberger ed., 1995) (1767).

7. *See* Bernard Mandeville, THE FABLE OF THE BEES AND OTHER WRITINGS (E.J. Hundert ed., 1997) (1723).

8. Adam Smith, THE WEALTH OF NATIONS: BOOKS IV–V 32 (Andrew Skinner ed., 1999) (1776).

9. Mancur Olson, THE LOGIC OF COLLECTIVE ACTION (1971).

10. Russell Hardin, *The Free Rider Problem, in* THE STANFORD ENCYCLOPEDIA OF PHILOSOPHY, http://plato.stanford.edu/entries/free-rider (2003).

11. Garrett Hardin, *The Tragedy of the Commons*, 162 SCIENCE 1243 (1968).

12. Although suggestions of the paradox go back to Mandeville's Fable of the Bees and even earlier, the first clear and extended statement may be John M. Robertson, THE PARADOX OF SAVING (1892). The best-known statement is John Maynard Keynes, THE GENERAL THEORY OF EMPLOYMENT, INTEREST AND MONEY 60 (1936) ("Every such attempt to save more by reducing consumption will so affect incomes that the attempt necessarily defeats itself"); see also Samuelson, *supra* note 5, at 270–272.

13. *See* Condorcet, *supra* note 2, at 52–56.

14. *See* Saul Levmore, *Public Choice Defended*, 72 U. CHI. L. REV. 777, 784 (2005) (reviewing Gerry Mackie, DEMOCRACY DEFENDED (2003)).

15. *See* Kenneth J. Arrow, SOCIAL CHOICE AND INDIVIDUAL VALUES 24–31, 51–59 (1st ed. 1951).

16. *See* Amartya Sen, RATIONALITY AND FREEDOM 69 n.5 (2002).

17. 3 James Bryce, THE AMERICAN COMMONWEALTH 119 (1st ed. 1888).

18. See Philip E. Converse, *Popular Representation and the Distribution of Information, in* INFORMATION AND DEMOCRATIC PROCESSES 369, 381–382 (John A. Ferejohn & James H. Kuklinski eds., 1990).

19. *See* 1 William Feller, AN INTRODUCTION TO PROBABILITY THEORY AND ITS APPLICATIONS 245 (3d ed. 1968).

20. *See* Condorcet, supra note 2, at 33, 48–49.

21. In fact, so long as the distribution of competence is symmetric around the mean in a group with three voters, the theorem can go through so long as the average chance of getting the right answer is greater than 0.471. *See*

Bernard Grofman et al., *Thirteen Theorems in Search of the Truth*, 15 THEORY & DECISION 261, 271 (1983).

22. *See* Condorcet, *supra* note 2, at 49.

23. *See* Scott E. Page, THE DIFFERENCE: HOW THE POWER OF DIVERSITY CREATES BETTER GROUPS, FIRMS, SCHOOLS, AND SOCIETIES 208–209 (2007); Krishna K. Ladha, *The Condorcet Jury Theorem, Free Speech, and Correlated Votes*, 36 AM. J. POL. SCI. 617, 625–630 (1992).

24. *See* Ladha, *supra* note 23, at 625–630.

25. For a survey of the literature, see generally Thomas J. Miles & Cass R. Sunstein, *The New Legal Realism*, 75 U. CHI. L. REV. 831 (2008).

26. *See* Kornhauser & Sager, *supra* note 3, at 3.

27. *See* Philip Pettit, *Deliberative Democracy and the Discursive Dilemma*, 11 PHILOSOPHICAL ISSUES 268 (2001); Christian List and Philip Pettit, *Aggregating Sets of Judgments: An Impossibility Result*, 18 ECON. & PHIL. 89 (2002).

28. See Lewis A. Kornhauser & Lawrence G. Sager, *Unpacking the Court*, 96 YALE L.J. 82, 102–105 (1986).

29. *See* List & Pettit, *supra* note 27, at 96–100 (considering procedures that met the following criteria: universal domain, anonymity, and systematicity).

30. *See* Dimitri Landa & Jeffrey R. Lax, *Legal Doctrine on Collegial Courts*, 71 J. POL. 946, 957–958 (2009).

31. *Id.*

32. David A. Strauss, *The Irrelevance of Constitutional Amendments*, 114 HARV. L. REV. 1457, 1459 (2001).

33. Strauss, *supra* note 32, at 1476–1477.

34. U.S. CONST. amend. XIV, § 1.

35. U.S. CONST. art. 4, § 2, cl. 1.

36. Strauss, *supra* note 32, at 1476–1478.

37. *Id.* at 1504.

38. *Id.* at 1481–1482.

39. *Id.* at 1484–1486.

40. *Id.* at 1475–1476.

41. See Frank H. Easterbrook, *Ways of Criticizing the Court*, 95 HARV. L. REV. 802, 815–817 (1982).

42. *See id.* at 817–821 ("Majority voting plus stare decisis is thus a formula under which the Court may produce any outcome favored by any number of Justices, however small, even though a majority of Justices would reject that rule ... on the basis of first principles." *Id.* at 819).

43. *See generally* William H. Riker, LIBERALISM AGAINST POPULISM (1982).
44. *See* Daniel A. Farber & Philip P. Frickey, LAW AND PUBLIC CHOICE: A CRITICAL INTRODUCTION 55.
45. *See* Maxwell L. Stearns, CONSTITUTIONAL PROCESS: A SOCIAL CHOICE ANALYSIS OF SUPREME COURT DECISION MAKING 54 (2000).
46. *See id.* at 53. Stearns's definition of the fallacy—as "the assumption that if phenomenon X produces result Y, more of phenomenon X will necessarily produce more of result Y"—is nonstandard, and would be more apt as a definition of an increasing function. However, the substance of Stearns's point holds straightforwardly, given the definition used here.
47. *See* Saul Levmore, *Bicameralism: When Are Two Decisions Better than One?*, 12 INT'L REV. L. & ECON. 145, 147 (1992).
48. *Id.*
49. See generally R.G. Lipsey & R.K. Lancaster, *The General Theory of Second Best*, 24 REV. ECON. STUD. 11 (1956).
50. *Id.* at 11–12.
51. *Id.*
52. For a similar example, see Thomas S. Ulen, *Courts, Legislatures, and the General Theory of Second Best in Law and Economics*, 73 CHI.-KENT L. REV. 189, 204–207 (1998).
53. The general theory of second best also shows that it is not necessarily best for the relevant variables to approach as closely as possible to their optimal values, assuming that at least one such variable does not reach the optimum. This mistake has been called the "approximation assumption." Avishai Margalit, *Ideals and Second Bests*, *in* PHILOSOPHY FOR EDUCATION 77, 77 (Seymour Fox ed., 1983).
54. For illuminating general discussions of the second best in legal theory, see Lawrence B. Solum, *Constitutional Possibilities*, 83 IND. L.J. 307, 311–312, 327–328 (2008); and Ulen, *supra* note 52, at 208–219. For illuminating discussions of the second best in political theory, see Jon Elster, EXPLAINING SOCIAL BEHAVIOR: MORE NUTS AND BOLTS FOR THE SOCIAL SCIENCES 439–442 (2007) [hereinafter Elster, EXPLAINING SOCIAL BEHAVIOR]; Bruce Talbot Coram, *Second Best Theories and the Implications for Institutional Design*, *in* THE THEORY OF INSTITUTIONAL DESIGN 90, 90–95 (Robert E. Goodin ed., 1996); Robert E. Goodin, *Political Ideals and Political Practice*, 25 BRIT. J. POL. SCI. 37, 52–55 (1995).
55. Polybius, THE RISE OF THE ROMAN EMPIRE 312–318 (Ian Scott-Kilvert trans., 1979).
56. Elster, EXPLAINING SOCIAL BEHAVIOR, *supra* note 54, at 440.

57. A.P. Thornton, Imperialism in the Twentieth Century 156 (1977); Adam B. Ulam, The Bolsheviks: The Intellectual and Political History of the Triumph of Communism in Russia 124–125, 137 (Harvard Univ. Press 1998) (1965); see also Elster, Explaining Social Behavior, *supra* note 54, at 440 (describing the rule of the Ottomans, the tsars in Russia, Mussolini in Italy, and Franco in Spain as "despotism tempered by incompetence" (internal quotation marks omitted)).

58. *See* David Hume, *Of the Independency of Parliament, in* Essays: Moral, Political, and Literary 42, 44–45 (Eugene F. Miller ed., 1985) (1777).

59. David Hume, *That Politics May Be Reduced to a Science, in* Essays: Moral, Political, and Literary, *supra* note 58, at 14, 18. The substance of Hume's reasoning is flawed, because in a hereditary monarchy the prospect of a crown may induce attempts to overthrow the reigning family through intrigue or violence.

60.
> "Their Laws and Clothes were equally
> Objects of Mutability;
> For, what was well done for a time,
> In half a Year became a Crime;
> Yet while they alter'd thus their Laws,
> Still finding and correcting Flaws,
> They mended by Inconstancy
> Faults, which no Prudence could foresee."

Mandeville, supra note 7, at 28.

61. 1 James Fitzjames Stephen, A History of the Criminal Law of England 284, 293 (1883).

62. Jane Mansbridge et al., *The Place of Self-Interest and the Role of Power in Deliberative Democracy*, 18 J. Pol. Phil. 64, 83 (2010).

63. Gary Lawson, *The Rise and Rise of the Administrative State*, 107 Harv. L. Rev. 1231, 1252–1253 (1994); Peter B. McCutchen, *Mistakes, Precedent, and the Rise of the Administrative State: Toward a Constitutional Theory of the Second Best*, 80 Cornell L. Rev. 1, 30–39 (1994).

64. *See* Martin S. Flaherty, *The Most Dangerous Branch*, 105 Yale L.J. 1725, 1828–1839 (1996); Abner S. Greene, *Checks and Balances in an Era of Presidential Lawmaking*, 61 U. Chi. L. Rev. 123, 155 (1994).

65. *See* Steven G. Calabresi, *Some Normative Arguments for the Unitary Executive*, 48 Ark. L. Rev. 23, 78–81 (1995); Robert Justin Lipkin, *The New Majoritarianism*, 69 U. Cin. L. Rev. 107, 121–122 (2000).

66. *See* Bruce Ackerman, *The New Separation of Powers*, 113 HARV. L. REV. 633, 656–657 (2000). There are significant scholarly controversies about whether presidentialism makes democracy unstable and whether proportional representation or fragmentation of parties also plays a role. *See,* e.g., José Antonio Cheibub, PRESIDENTIALISM, PARLIAMENTARIANISM, AND DEMOCRACY (2007). For present purposes, the substance of these controversies is irrelevant; what matters is the second-best structure of the argument.

67. This is Duverger's Law. *See* Maurice Duverger, POLITICAL PARTIES: THEIR ORGANIZATION AND ACTIVITY IN THE MODERN STATE 217 (Barbara North & Robert North trans., John Wiley & Sons 3d Eng. ed., rev., 1963) (1951).

68. James M. Landis, THE ADMINISTRATIVE PROCESS 46 (1938).

69. *See* Lawrence Lessig & Cass R. Sunstein, *The President and the Administration*, 94 COLUM. L. REV. 1, 2–3 (1994).

70. *Id.* at 81–87, 97–101.

71. Elster, EXPLAINING SOCIAL BEHAVIOR, *supra* note 54, at 439.

72. Alexander M. Bickel, THE MORALITY OF CONSENT 87 (1975). For an illuminating critique, see Note, *Media Incentives and National Security Secrets*, 122 HARV. L. REV. 2228 (2009).

73. This seems to be Bickel's implicit argument. *See* Bickel, *supra* note 72, at 81–87.

74. *See* James Fitzjames Stephen, A GENERAL VIEW OF THE CRIMINAL LAW OF ENGLAND 166 (1863) (arguing that although "the inquisitorial theory of criminal procedure is beyond all question the true one," nonetheless "it may be, and probably is, the case, that in our own time and country, the best manner of conducting such an inquiry is to consider the trial mainly as a litigation, and to allow each party to say all that can be said in support of their own view").

75. *See* Antonin Scalia, *Originalism: The Lesser Evil*, 57 U. CIN. L. REV. 849, 864 (1989).

76. *Id.*

77. *See* Lawrence Lessig, *Fidelity in Translation*, 71 TEX. L. REV. 1165, 1171–1173, 1189–1192 (1993).

78. Lawrence Lessig, *Translating Federalism:* United States v. Lopez, 1995 SUP. CT. REV. 125, 193.

79. At least if we bracket the possibility that the analyst is engaged in what David Estlund calls "hopeless aspirational theory"; such analysts, Estlund argues, can ignore problems of the second best. See David Estlund,

Utopophobia (February 9, 2009) (unpublished manuscript, on file with the Harvard Law School Library). I will put aside the possibility of hopeless theorizing in what follows.

CHAPTER 2

1. An important exception is Jenna Bednar's systemic analysis of federalism. *See generally* Jenna Bednar, THE ROBUST FEDERATION (2009).
2. THE FEDERALIST NO. 51, at 318–319 (James Madison) (Clinton Rossiter ed., 1999).
3. For Adam Smith's influence on Madison, see David Prindle, *The Invisible Hand of James Madison*, 15 CONST. POL. ECON. 223 (2004).
4. Edna Ullmann-Margalit, *The Invisible Hand and the Cunning of Reason*, 64 SOC. RES. 181, 182 (1997).
5. Prindle, *supra* note 3, at 231–234.
6. THE FEDERALIST NO. 51 (James Madison), supra note 2, at 319.
7. *See* Daryl J. Levinson, *Empire-Building Government in Constitutional Law*, 118 HARV. L. REV. 915, 923–937 (2005) [hereinafter Levinson, *Empire-Building Government*].
8. THE FEDERALIST NO. 51 (James Madison), *supra* note 2, at 319.
9. *See* Levinson, *Empire-Building Government, supra* note 7, at 920.
10. For some conjectures on how such alignment occurred in Eastern Europe, see Jon Elster, *The Role of Institutional Interest in East European Constitution-Making*, 5 E. EUR. CONST. REV. 63 (1996).
11. *See* Adam Smith, THE WEALTH OF NATIONS: BOOKS IV–V 32 (Andrew Skinner ed., 1999) (1776).
12. *See* Eric A. Posner & Adrian Vermeule, *Constitutional Showdowns*, 156 U. PA. L. REV. 991, 1032–1033 (2008).
13. *See, e.g.,* John O. McGinnis, *Constitutional Review by the Executive in Foreign Affairs and War Powers: A Consequence of Rational Choice in the Separation of Powers*, 56 LAW & CONTEMP. PROBS, at 293, 303 (1993); John O. McGinnis, *The Spontaneous Order of War Powers*, 47 CASE W. RES. L. REV. 1317, 1326 (1997).
14. For an analysis of divide-and-conquer tactics, see Eric A. Posner, Kathryn E. Spier & Adrian Vermeule, *Divide and Conquer*, 2 J. LEGAL ANALYSIS 417 (2010). A version of the following discussion is included in that paper.
15. David Hume, *Of the Independency of Parliament*, in ESSAYS: MORAL, POLITICAL, AND LITERARY, 42, at 42, 44 (Eugene F. Miller ed., 1985) (1777).
16. *Id.* at 45.

17. Applying Eric Rasmusen & J. Mark Ramseyer, *Cheap Bribes and the Corruption Ban: A Coordination Game Among Rational Legislators*, 78 PUB. CHOICE 305, 309–313 (1994).

18. *Id.* at 313. For similar models of divide-and-conquer tactics in other settings, see Ilya Segal, *Contracting with Externalities*, 114 Q. J. ECON. 337, 343 (1999); Ilya Segal, *Coordination and Discrimination in Contracting with Externalities: Divide and Conquer?*, 113 J. ECON. THEORY 147, 153–155 (2003); and Yeon-Koo Che & Kathryn E. Spier, *Exploiting Plaintiffs Through Settlement: Divide and Conquer*, 164 J. INSTITUTIONAL AND THEORETICAL ECON. 4 (2008).

19. This feature of discriminatory vote-buying offers tracks the logic of divide-and-conquer models in other areas, in which discriminatory offers allow the single party on one side of the transaction to exclude equilibria in which the multiple parties on the other side of the transaction coordinate for mutual gain. For a general model, see Posner, Spier & Vermeule, *Divide and Conquer, supra* note 14.

20. Applying the ingenious model in Ernesto Dal Bó, *Bribing Voters*, 51 AM. J. POL. SCI. 789, 791–795 (2007).

21. *See id.* at 793.

22. More specifically, a sum equal to the individual costs to the pivotal voter if the Crown's proposal is enacted plus a token amount, in order to make the pivotal voter prefer that it be enacted. *See id.* at 794.

23. *See id.* at 793–794.

24. *See id.* at 792.

25. *See id.*

26. David Hume, *Whether the British Government Inclines More to Absolute Monarchy, or to a Republic, in* ESSAYS: MORAL, POLITICAL, AND LITERARY, *supra* note 15, at 47, 48.

27. Charles A. Beard, AMERICAN GOVERNMENT AND POLITICS 470–471 (1st ed. 1911).

28. *Id.*

29. *See,* e.g., Jerry L. Mashaw, GREED, CHAOS, AND GOVERNANCE 152 (1997).

30. *See* Jide Nzelibe, *The Fable of the Nationalist President and the Parochial Congress*, 53 UCLA L. REV. 1217, 1221, 1231–1242 (2006).

31. *See id.* at 1235–1242. These are just possibilities or hypotheses that I discuss for analytic clarity. The best current evidence, although not airtight, suggests that since World War II, "the median constituencies of the House and Senate have approximated the presidential constituency as well as

each other," albeit with the House and Senate showing a very slight Republican skew. David R. Mayhew, Partisan Balance: Why Political Parties Don't Kill the U.S. Constitutional System xix (2011). Each constituency is thus an approximate "microcosm" of the national electorate as a whole. *Id.*

32. Torsten Persson, Gérard Roland & Guido Tabellini, *Separation of Powers and Political Accountability*, 112 Q. J. Econ. 1163, 1179–1183 (1997).

33. *Id.* at 1182–1183.

34. Saul Levmore, *Bicameralism: When Are Two Decisions Better than One?*, 12 Int'l Rev. L. & Econ. 145, 147–148 (1992).

35. James R. Rogers, *An Information Rationale for Congruent Bicameralism*, 13(2) J. Theoretical Politics 125 (2001).

36. James M. Buchanan & Gordon Tullock, The Calculus of Consent (1962), *reprinted in* 3 The Collected Works of James M. Buchanan 220 (1999).

37. *Id.* at 233–234, 239–240.

38. *Cf.* Loving v. United States, 517 U.S. 748, 757–758 (1996) (describing bicameralism as a feature of Congress that makes for "responsive" lawmaking).

39. *See* Buchanan & Tullock, *supra* note 36, at 233–234.

40. Robert A. Dahl, How Democratic Is the American Constitution? (2002).

41. Sanford Levinson, Our Undemocratic Constitution 172–173 (2006) [hereinafter Levinson, Undemocratic Constitution].

42. *Id.* at 50–51.

43. *Id.* at 87–88.

44. *Id.* at 125, 136–137.

45. *See id.* at 8–9, 27–29, 49.

46. Levinson, Undemocratic Constitution, *supra* note 41, at 49.

47. *See id.* at 50–52.

48. *Id.* at 88–89.

49. *See* Andrew Gelman et al., *The Mathematics and Statistics of Voting Power*, 17 Stat. Sci. 420, 426–428 (2002).

50. Levinson, Undemocratic Constitution, *supra* note 41, at 52.

51. *Id.* at 109–116; *id.* at 167 (listing "[e]xcessive presidential power" as a "grievous defect[]" of the Constitution).

52. *See id., supra* note 41, at 89–91.

53. Dahl, *supra* note 40, at 68–72.

54. *Cf.* James M. Landis, The Administrative Process 46 (1938).

55. *Id.* at 1 (arguing that "the administrative process springs from the inadequacy of a simple tripartite form of government to deal with modern problems").

56. *See, e.g.,* Samuel Issacharoff, *Gerrymandering and Political Cartels,* 116 HARV. L. REV. 593, 617–630 (2002).

57. *See* Nathaniel Persily, *Reply: In Defense of Foxes Guarding Henhouses: The Case for Judicial Acquiescence to Incumbent-Protecting Gerrymanders,* 116 HARV. L. REV. 649, 668 (2002).

58. *Id.*

59. Heather K. Gerken, *Second-Order Diversity,* 118 HARV. L. REV. 1099, 1117–1118 (2005).

60. Nancy L. Rosenblum, ON THE SIDE OF THE ANGELS: AN APPRECIATION OF PARTIES AND PARTISANSHIP 456–457 (2008).

61. Justin Fox & Richard van Weelden, *Partisanship and the Effectiveness of Oversight,* 94 JOURNAL OF PUBLIC ECONOMICS 674, 674 (2010).

62. *See* Vicki C. Jackson, *Narratives of Federalism: Of Continuities and Comparative Constitutional Experience,* 51 DUKE L.J. 223, 226, 272–279 (2001); *see also* Mikhail Filippov, Peter C. Ordeshook & Olga Shvetsova, DESIGNING FEDERALISM: A THEORY OF SELF-SUSTAINABLE FEDERAL INSTITUTIONS 300–301 (2004) (emphasizing that, because institutions are interdependent, the constitutional designer cannot evaluate them piecemeal). Thanks to Mark Tushnet for these references.

63. *See* Adrian Vermeule, LAW AND THE LIMITS OF REASON 170–171 (2009); Heather K. Gerken, *The Hydraulics of Constitutional Reform: A Skeptical Response to Our Undemocratic Constitution,* 55 DRAKE L. REV. 925, 927 n.14 (2007).

64. Alexander M. Bickel, THE LEAST DANGEROUS BRANCH: THE SUPREME COURT AT THE BAR OF POLITICS 16 (2d ed. 1986).

65. *See generally* Jeremy Waldron, LAW AND DISAGREEMENT (1999); Jeremy Waldron, *The Core of the Case Against Judicial Review,* 115 YALE L.J. 1346 (2006). For an important line of critique, see Frank B. Cross, *Institutions and Enforcement of the Bill of Rights,* 85 CORNELL L. REV. 1529, 1550–1576 (2000); and Richard H. Fallon, Jr., *The Core of an Uneasy Case for Judicial Review,* 121 HARV. L. REV. 1693 (2008).

66. John Hart Ely, DEMOCRACY AND DISTRUST: A THEORY OF JUDICIAL REVIEW 73–104 (1980).

67. *See* Cross, *supra* note 65, at 1550–1576; Fallon, *supra* note 65, at 1718–1728.

68. I believe that robust judicial review cannot, in fact, be justified in such terms, *see* Adrian Vermeule, JUDGING UNDER UNCERTAINTY: AN

Institutional Theory of Legal Interpretation (2006), but that is a separate question.

69. Frederick Schauer, *The Supreme Court, 2005 Term—Foreword: The Court's Agenda—And the Nation's*, 120 Harv. L. Rev. 4 (2006).

70. Schauer also briefly discusses the Court's statutory agenda, but the main implications he elicits are addressed to constitutional theory, so I shall focus on his discussion of the Court's constitutional agenda. *Id.*

71. *Id.* at 50.

72. *Id.* at 53.

73. I take this phrase from Mark Tushnet, Taking the Constitution Away from the Courts 57 (1999), who uses it in a somewhat different sense, although a related one.

74. Schauer, *supra* note 69, at 53. Schauer limits his argument by saying that the Court should intervene primarily on "low-salience" questions. *See id.* at 36–62. This limitation partially but not wholly avoids the problem noted in the text, because it will be uncertain ex ante when the limitation applies.

75. 128 S. Ct. 2229 (2008).

76. I will ignore "personal" bias, which arises when rulings are based on bribery or family connections.

77. Thomas J. Miles & Cass R. Sunstein, *The New Legal Realism*, 75 U. Chi. L. Rev. 831 (2008).

78. $((8 \times .5) + 1) / 9 \approx .56$.

79. This is calculated according to the following formula: probability = (number of scenarios in which 4, 5, 6, 7, or 8 partisan justices vote correctly) / (total number of scenarios) = $(_8C_4 + _8C_5 + _8C_6 + _8C_7 + _8C_8) / (2^8) = (70 + 56 + 28 + 8 + 1) / 256 \approx .64$. Thanks to Joanna Huey and John Polley for this calculation.

80. Thomas J. Miles & Cass R. Sunstein, *Do Judges Make Regulatory Policy? An Empirical Investigation of* Chevron, 73 U. Chi. L. Rev. 823, 834 (2006). This study, however, does not include Chief Justice Roberts or Justices Alito and Sotomayor. A subsequent study, conducted in 2008, found that Justice Kennedy provided the fifth vote in four administrative law decisions that came before the Roberts Court: three of these gave the conservative bloc the majority, while one gave the liberal bloc the majority. *See* Ann Graham, *Searching for* Chevron *in Muddy* Watters: *The Roberts Court and Judicial Review of Agency Regulations*, 60 Admin. L. Rev. 229, 266 (2008).

81. *See* Charlie Savage, *Appeals Courts Pushed to Right by Bush Choices*, N.Y. Times, October 29, 2008, at A1.

82. *See* Eric A. Posner, *Does Political Bias in the Judiciary Matter?: Implications of Judicial Bias Studies for Legal and Constitutional Reform*, 75 U. CHI. L. REV. 853, 858–868 (2008). *See generally* James R. Rogers & Georg Vanberg, *Resurrecting* Lochner: *A Defense of Unprincipled Judicial Activism*, 23 J.L. ECON. & ORG. 442 (2007).

83. *Cf.* Posner, *supra* note 82, at 855 ("[J]udicial bias (within limits) does not matter at all and could even be beneficial in a system…where judges are expected to block or restrict government actions…that are themselves likely to reflect 'bias'") (emphasis omitted).

84. *See id.* at 879.

85. *Cf. id.* at 880 ("If legislative bias yields inefficient and unfair statutes because the legislative process is insufficiently supermajoritarian, and if legislative bargaining costs are low, then review of statutes by biased judges may be socially desirable").

86. *See, e.g.,* Miles & Sunstein, *supra* note 80, at 851–859; Richard L. Revesz, *Environmental Regulation, Ideology, and the D.C. Circuit*, 83 VA. L. REV. 1717, 1719 (1997). For a recent overview of the literature on panel effects, see Pauline T. Kim, *Deliberation and Strategy on the United States Courts of Appeals: An Empirical Exploration of Panel Effects*, 157 U. PA. L. REV. 1319, 1320–1327 (2009); for the effect of court composition on the behavior of individual Supreme Court justices, see Scott R. Meinke and Kevin M. Scott, *Collegial Influence and Judicial Voting Change: The Effect of Membership Change on U.S. Supreme Court Justices*, 41 L. & SOC'Y REV. 909 (2007); and for the effect of court composition on the behavior of individual circuit judges, see Todd Collins, *Is the Sum Greater than Its Parts? Circuit Court Composition and Judicial Behavior in the Courts of Appeals*, 32 L. & POL'Y 434 (2010).

CHAPTER 3

1. There is a large literature on what exactly Smith meant by his evocative, but unsystematic, references to the "invisible hand," and how exactly his metaphor relates to modern economics. *See, e.g.,* William D. Grampp, *What Did Adam Smith Mean by the Invisible Hand?*, 108 J. POL. ECON. 441, 444–450 (2000). Nothing in the analysis here turns on how such questions are answered.

2. F. A. Hayek, *The Use of Knowledge in Society*, 35 AM. ECON. REV. 519, 524–526 (1945).

3. THE FEDERALIST NO. 51 at 356 (James Madison) (Benjamin F. Wright ed., 1961). For the influence of Smith on Madison, see David Prindle, *The*

Invisible Hand of James Madison, 15 Const. POL. ECON. 223 (2004). *See also* Samuel Fleischacker, *Adam Smith's Reception among the American Founders, 1776–1790*, 59 Wm. & MARY Q. (2002).

4. *See* John O. McGinnis, *Constitutional Review by the Executive in Foreign Affairs and War Powers: A Consequence of Rational Choice in the Separation of Powers*, 56 LAW & CONTEMP. PROBS, at 293, 303 (1993) (1993).

5. *See* FEDERALIST NO. 51 (James Madison) (Isaac Kramnick ed., 1987) at 322 ("In the extended republic of the United States, and among the great variety of interests, parties and sects which it embraces, a coalition of a majority of the whole society could rarely take place on any other principles than those of justice and the general good"). For Madison's debt to Hume, see Nancy L. Rosenblum, ON THE SIDE OF THE ANGELS: AN APPRECIATION OF PARTIES AND PARTISANSHIP 70–71 (2008).

6. *See* FEDERALIST NO. 10 (Madison) (Isaac Kramnick ed., 1987) at 128; James Madison, *Parties, in* JAMES MADISON: WRITINGS (Jack Rakove ed., 1999) 504–505. Madison's pluralism was sharply qualified: he distinguished "natural" from "artificial" parties, and argued that "the expediency, in politics, of making natural parties, mutual checks on each other" did not support creating artificial parties "in order to form them into mutual checks." *Id.* at 505. Because the checking solution is a second-best remedy adopted only because natural parties are "unavoidable," *id.* at 504, that solution is not to be affirmatively chosen where necessity does not require it.

7. *See* THE FEDERALIST NO. 51, at 318–319 (James Madison) (Clinton Rossiter ed., 1999).

8. John Stuart Mill, ON LIBERTY (1859).

9. Abrams v. United States, 250 U.S. 616, 630 (1919) (Holmes, J., dissenting).

10. Alexander M. Bickel, THE MORALITY OF CONSENT 81–88 (1975).

11. Frank H. Easterbrook, *Criminal Procedure as a Market System*, 12 J. LEGAL STUD. 289, 292–298 (1983).

12. James Fitzjames Stephen, A GENERAL VIEW OF THE CRIMINAL LAW OF ENGLAND 166 (1863).

13. *See, e.g.,* Monroe H. Freedman & Abbe Smith, UNDERSTANDING LAWYERS' ETHICS 119–122 (3rd ed. 2004).

14. See references and discussion in sources cited infra notes 49, 56.

15. Paul H. Rubin, *Why is the Common Law Efficient?*, 6 J. LEGAL STUD. 51, 53–55 (1977); *see also* George L. Priest, *The Common Law Process and the Selection of Efficient Rules*, 6 J. LEGAL STUD. 65, 66–69 (1977); for an

overview of the large literature, see Paul H. Rubin, *Macro and Micro Legal Efficiency: Supply and Demand*, 13 SUP. CT. ECON. REV. 19 (2005).

16. Nicola Gennaioli & Andrei Shleifer, *The Evolution of Common Law*, 115 J. POL. ECON. 43, 60–61 (2007).

17. Harold Demsetz, *Toward a Theory of Property Rights*, 57 AM. ECON. REV. 347 (1967).

18. Thomas W. Merrill, *The Demsetz Thesis and the Evolution of Property Rights*, 31 J. LEG. STUD. S331, S331 (2002).

19. Demsetz, *supra* note 17, at 350.

20. *See, e.g.*, James E. Krier, *Evolutionary Theory and the Origin of Property Rights*, 95 CORNELL L. REV. 139 (2009).

21. The agents might be individuals or instead institutional actors, such as states in international relations theory, or lawmaking institutions in the Madisonian invisible-hand account of the separation of powers. Methodological individualists will add that the behavior of the institutions is in principle reducible to statements about individuals, but for my purposes the validity of this claim is irrelevant.

22. Edna Ullmann-Margalit, *Invisible-Hand Explanations*, 39 SYNTHESE 263, 270 (1978).

23. Robert Nozick, ANARCHY, STATE, AND UTOPIA 18–19 (1974).

24. Ullmann-Margalit, *supra* note 22, at 265.

25. Ullmann-Margalit, *supra* note 22, at 275.

26. Justin Wolfers and Eric Zitzewitz, *Prediction Markets*, 18 J. ECON. PERSP. 107, 122 (2004) (citing Kay-Yut Chen & Charles Plott, *Information-Aggregation Mechanisms: Concept, Design and Implementation for a Sales Forecasting Problem* (Cal. Inst. Tech. Social Science Working Paper No. 1131, 2002)); Note, *Prediction Markets and Law: A Skeptical Account*, 122 HARV. L. REV. 1217, 1221 (2009).

27. Robert Sugden, *Spontaneous Order*, 3 J. ECON. Persp. 85, 93–94 (1989).

28. Amartya Sen, RATIONALITY AND FREEDOM 501–530 (2002).

29. FEDERALIST NO. 51 (James Madison), *supra* note 7.

30. However, because market participants have incentives to free-ride on the information generated by others, full informational efficiency in markets is impossible. *See* Sanford J. Grossman & Joseph E. Stiglitz, *On the Impossibility of Informationally Efficient Markets*, 70 AM. ECON. REV. 393 (1980).

31. *See* Grampp, *supra* note 1, at 445–446.

32. *See* Easterbrook, *supra* note 11.

33. *Id.*
34. *See* Richard A. Posner, Economic Analysis of Law 223 (7th ed. 2007).
35. *See* Merrill, *supra* note 18, at S336–S337. For the point that property rights may not evolve toward efficiency because of interest-group pressures, see Saul Levmore, *Two Stories about the Evolution of Property Rights*, 31 J. Leg. Stud. S421 (2002).
36. For references and an overview of the problems, see Adrian Vermeule, Law and the Limits of Reason 106–107 (2009).
37. *See* Prindle, *supra* note 3; Fleischacker, *supra* note 3.
38. *See* Eric A. Posner & Adrian Vermeule, *Constitutional Showdowns*, 156 U. Pa. L. Rev. 991, 1032–1033 (2008).
39. *See, e.g.*, Torsten Persson, Gérard Roland & Guido Tabellini, *Separation of Powers and Political Accountability*, 112 Q.J. Econ. 1163 (1997).
40. *See* Geoffrey Brennan and Alan Hamlin, *A Revisionist View of the Separation of Powers*, 6 J. Theoretical Pol. 345 (1994).
41. On the divergence between institutional and individual interests, see Daryl J. Levinson, *Empire-Building Government in Constitutional Law*, 118 Harv. L. Rev. 915, 923–937, 951–953 (2005).
42. Jon Elster, Ulysses Unbound: Studies in Rationality, Precommitment, and Constraints 58, 94–95 (2000).
43. Daron Acemoglu, *Why Not a Political Coase Theorem? Social Conflict, Commitment, and Politics*, 31 J. Comp. Econ. 620, 622–623, 638 (2003).
44. Bradford R. Clark, *Separation of Powers as a Safeguard of Federalism*, 79 Tex. L. Rev. 1321, 1459 (2001).
45. McGinnis acknowledges that the "spontaneous order" arising from the separation of powers is unlikely to promote either liberty or social welfare as a general matter. *See* McGinnis, *supra* note 4, at 303.
46. Ullmann-Margalit, *supra* note 22, at 274.
47. *See* Wolfers and Zitzewitz, *supra* note 26.
48. The literature on these issues is vast. Clear treatments are Jon Elster, The Cement of Society (1989); Eric A. Posner, Law and Social Norms (2002).
49. Arthur Isak Applbaum, Ethics for Adversaries: The Morality of Roles in Public and Professional Life 196 (1999). This sort of view may or may not be combined with the further thesis that in the long run, markets themselves tend to undermine the norms on which the efficient functioning of markets depends—what has been dubbed the thesis of "parasitic liberalism." See Samuel Bowles, *Is Liberal Society a Parasite on*

Tradition?, 39 PHIL. PUB. AFF. 46 (2011). For a classic statement of the thesis, see Daniel Bell, CULTURAL CONTRADICTIONS OF CAPITALISM (1976).

50. Kenneth J. Arrow, *Social Responsibility and Economic Efficiency*, 21 PUB. POL'Y 303, 313–315 (1973) [hereinafter Arrow, *Social Responsibility*].

51. George A. Akerlof, *The Market for "Lemons": Quality Uncertainty and the Market Mechanism*, 84 Q.J. ECON. 488, 489–491, 495 (1970).

52. Kenneth J. Arrow, *Gifts and Exchanges*, 1 PHIL. PUB. AFF. 343, 345 (1972).

53. Rosenblum, *supra* note 5, at 125.

54. *Id.* at 10.

55. William Nelson, *The Free Speech/Free Market Analogy: A Comment on Steven Lee* 4 (unpublished ms. 2008).

56. Gary Goodpaster, *On the Theory of American Adversary Criminal Trial*, 78 J. CRIM. L. & CRIMINOLOGY 118, 121–124 (1987).

57. Albert O. Hirschman, *Rival Views of Market Society, in* RIVAL VIEWS OF MARKET SOCIETY AND OTHER RECENT ESSAYS 105, 124–132 (1986).

58. Arrow, *Gifts and Exchanges*, supra note 52.

59. The tension between altruism and reciprocity is identified in Sung-Ha Hwang and Samuel Bowles, *Is Altruism Bad for Cooperation?* (unpublished ms).

60. See Ernst Fehr and Urs Fischbacher, *Third Party Punishment and Social Norms*, 25 EVOL. & HUM. BEHAVIOR 63–87 (2004).

61. Cass R. Sunstein, *Government Control of Information*, 74 CAL. L. REV. 889, 902 (1986) (emphasis added).

62. Arrow, *Gifts and Exchanges, supra* note 52, at 354–355.

63. *See* Arrow, *Social Responsibility, supra* note 50, at 304–309.

64. Adam Smith, THE WEALTH OF NATIONS: BOOK I, CH. X (Andrew Skinner ed., 1999) (1776).

65. Arrow, *Gifts and Exchanges, supra* note 52, at 354.

66. *See also* Arrow, *Social Responsibility, supra* note 50, at 316 ("Ethical codes, if they are to be viable, should be limited in their scope [to situations of market failure]"). Which institutions or individuals will have both the capacity and the incentive to do the limiting is unclear.

67. Gordon S. Bergsten, *On the Role of Social Norms in a Market Economy*, 45 PUBLIC CHOICE 113, 113 (1985) (arguing that the normative economic theory of social norms "is flawed because it is not grounded in an understanding of the processes by which social norms are created, maintained and enforced"). More recent work has in a sense corrected this problem, by elaborating models of the supply side of norms, and in another sense

has exacerbated it, by showing that the resulting norms need not be efficient. See generally Posner, *supra* note 48; Sugden, *supra* note 27.

68. Sugden, *supra* note 27, at 93.

69. See Posner, *supra* note 48, at 169–179.

70. Robert C. Ellickson, ORDER WITHOUT LAW: HOW NEIGHBORS SETTLE DISPUTES 153–154, 167–168 (1991); *The Market for Social Norms*, 3 AM. L. & ECON. REV. 1, 31–35 (2001). For an attempt to identify possible mechanisms supporting norm-enforcement in broader groups, see Lior Jacob Strahilevitz, *Social Norms from Close-Knit Groups to Loose-Knit Groups*, 70 U. CHI. L. REV. 359 (2003).

71. The belief that any movement toward the systemic optimum, short of full attainment, is nonetheless desirable has been called the "approximation assumption": the fallacious view that the best course of action is the one that approximates an unobtainable ideal as closely as possible. See Avishai Margalit, *Ideals and Second Bests, in* PHILOSOPHY FOR EDUCATION, 77 (Seymour Fox ed., 1983).

72. *See* Jon Elster, *The Market and the Forum: Three Varieties of Political Theory, in* FOUNDATIONS OF SOCIAL CHOICE THEORY 103, 115–116 (Jon Elster & Aanund Hylland eds., 1986).

73. Elster, *supra* note 72, at 115–116 (quoting Raymond Smullyan, THIS BOOK NEEDS NO TITLE: A BUDGET OF LIVING PARADOXES 56 (1980)).

74. Serge-Christophe Kolm, *Altruism and Efficiency*, 94 ETHICS 18, 33–34 (1983).

75. See Rosenblum, *supra* note 5.

76. William Butler Yeats, "The Second Coming" (1920).

77. For an overview of these limitations, see John E. Finn, *Electoral Regimes and the Proscription of Anti-democratic Parties, in* THE DEMOCRATIC EXPERIENCE AND POLITICAL VIOLENCE 51, 71 (David C. Rapoport & Leonard Weinberg eds., 2001).

78. I will bracket here all questions about the *internal* aggregation of preferences within institutions, and assume that the institutions can be understood as having something like composite utility functions. On the problems of internal aggregation, see generally Levinson, *Empire-Making Government, supra* note 41.

79. Peter M. Shane, *When Inter-Branch Norms Break Down: Of Arms-for-Hostages, "Orderly Shutdowns," Presidential Impeachments, and Judicial "Coups,"* 12 CORNELL J.L. & PUB. POL'Y 503, 508 (2003).

80. Robert H. Jackson, The Federal Prosecutor, Address at the Second Annual Conference of United States Attorneys, (April 1, 1940), in NATIONAL

College of District Attorneys, Ethical Considerations in
Prosecution: Roles and Functions of the Prosecutor 2 (John
J. Douglass ed., 1977).

81. Cf. William H. Simon, The Practice of Justice: A Theory of
Lawyers' Ethics 9–10, 138–139 (1998) ("the lawyer should take such
action as, considering the relevant circumstances of the particular case,
seems likely to promote justice").

82. See H. Richard Uviller, *The Neutral Prosecutor: The Obligation of Dispassion
in a Passionate Pursuit*, 68 Fordham L. Rev. 1695, 1716 (2000).

83. For the many different versions of this ratio in various times and places,
see Alexander Volokh, *n Guilty Men*, 146 U. Pa. L. Rev. 173 (1997).

84. This assumes informative voting, in which jurors vote in accordance with
their individual evidentiary signals. With strategic voting, in which jurors
draw information from the votes of other jurors, increasing the size of the
jury may actually increase the chances of a unanimous verdict for an erroneous conviction. Jurors will reason that if they are pivotal under a una-
nimity rule, every other juror is voting to convict; and the larger the number
of jurors, the more powerful this inference becomes. See Timothy Feddersen
and Wolfgang Pesendorfer, *Convicting the Innocent: The Inferiority of
Unanimous Jury Verdicts under Strategic Voting*, 92 Am. Pol. Sci. Rev. 23
(1998). However, experiments do not bear out this counterintuitive thesis,
and indeed "the gap between the theoretical prediction and the experimental data [grows] with jury size." Arthur Lupia et. al., *When Should
Political Scientists Use the Self-Confirming Equilibrium Concept? Benefits, Costs
and an Application to Jury Theorems* 23 (unpublished ms).

85. For an overview of Assurance games in which players have incomplete
information about others' preferences, see Andrew H. Kydd, Trust and
Mistrust in International Relations ch. 2 (2005).

86. In this sort of *self-confirming equilibrium*, players' conjectures about other
players' strategies are confirmed so long as the conjectures match the
other players' actual behavior under the actual circumstances, as opposed
to their counterfactual behavior under different circumstances. See Lupia
et al., *supra* note 84.

87. *See* Sunstein, *supra* note 61, at 904; *see also* Note, *Media Incentives and
National Security Secrets*, 122 Harv. L. Rev. 2228, 2233–2234 (2009).

88. Frederick Schauer, Free Speech: A Philosophical Enquiry 26 (1982).

89. Goodpaster, *supra* note 56, at 124.

90. F.A. Hayek, *Der Wettbewerb als Entdeckungsverfahren*, Institut für
Weltwirtschaft Lecture at the University of Kiel (1968), translated as

Competition as a Discovery Procedure, 5 Q.J. AUSTRIAN ECON. 9 (Marcellus S. Snow trans., 2002). For an application to legal institutions, see Gregory B. Christainsen, *Law as a Discovery Procedure*, 9 CATO J. 497 (1990).

91. Hayek, *supra* note 90, at 9–10 (emphasis in original). Hayek may be wrong to put games into this category. Games, unlike examinations, may not be best understood as a means of uncovering independent information; if the game is played according to its rules, the outcome is necessarily correct. However, I am unsure of this point. It seems perfectly coherent to affirm both that the point of the annual Wimbledon tennis tournament is to determine who is the best tennis player at a given time, and also that in a particular year, the winner of the tournament was not the best player.

92. David Luban, *The Adversary System Excuse, in* THE GOOD LAWYER: LAWYERS' ROLES AND LAWYERS' ETHICS, 83, 93 (David Luban ed., 1983).

93. Luban, *supra* note 92, at 94.

94. Cf. Ullmann-Margalit, *supra* note 22, at 267–268.

95. Hayek, *supra* note 90, at 10 (Marcellus S. Snow trans., 2002) (emphasis added).

96. Discussed in Cass R. Sunstein, WHY SOCIETIES NEED DISSENT 146–148 (2003).

97. *See generally* Friedrich A. Hayek, LAW, LEGISLATION AND LIBERTY, VOL. I: RULES AND ORDER (1973); for a summary and critique, see Gerald F. Gaus, *Hayek on the Evolution of Society and Mind, in* THE CAMBRIDGE COMPANION TO HAYEK 232 (Edward Feser ed., 2006).

98. Luban, *supra* note 92, at 93.

99. Mark J. Roe, *Chaos and Evolution in Law and Economics*, 109 HARV. L. REV. 641, 664 (1996).

100. John Roemer, A FUTURE FOR SOCIALISM 3 (1994). See also Roe, *supra* note 99, at 665.

101. A large body of literature claims that the common law produces superior economic performance. *See* Edward L. Glaeser & Andrei Shleifer, *Legal Origins*, 117 Q.J. ECON. 1193, 1194 (2002); Paul G. Mahoney, *The Common Law and Economic Growth: Hayek Might Be Right*, 30 J. LEGAL STUD. 503, 514–519 (2001). More recently, however, leading proponents of this thesis have modified the claim to say that a general free-market orientation—which "even legislation in common law countries [may express]"—is the causal factor. Rafael LaPorta, Florencio Lopez-de-Silanes & Andrei Shleifer, *The Economic Consequences of Legal Origins*, 46 J. ECON. LIT. 285, 291 (2008).

102. Jon Elster, Explaining Social Behavior: More Nuts and Bolts for the Social Sciences (2007).

CHAPTER 4

1. The problem of "selection effects" I discuss here should not be confused with the problem of selection effects in statistical inference. In law, another common usage of the phrase involves changes in the pool of litigated cases that result from settlement decisions. *See* George Priest & Benjamin Klein, *The Selection of Disputes for Litigation*, 6(1) J. Legal Stud. 65 (1977).

2. *See generally* Donella H. Meadows, Thinking in Systems: A Primer (2008).

3. For a lucid overview of the burgeoning literature in political science, see Timothy Besley, *Political Selection*, 19(3) J. Econ. Persp. 43 (2005).

4. Robert D. Cooter, *Who Gets On Top in Democracy? Elections as Filters*, 10 Sup. Ct. Econ. Rev. 127 (2003).

5. *See* The Federalist No. 57, at 318 (James Madison) (Clinton Rossiter ed.): "[The] aim of every political constitution is, or ought to be, first to obtain for rulers men who possess most wisdom to discern, and most virtue to pursue, the common good of society; and in the next place, to take the most effectual precautions for keeping them virtuous whilst they continue to hold the public trust."

6. The literature pursuing this theme is vast. For an important recent example, see John Ferejohn, *Accountability and Authority: Toward a Theory of Political Accountability, in* Democracy, Accountability and Representation 131 (Adam Przeworski, Susan C. Stokes & Bernard Manin eds., 1999).

7. David Hume, *Of the Independency of Parliament, in* Essays: Moral, Political, and Literary (Eugene F. Miller, ed, Liberty Fund, 1985) (1741).

8. Anthony Downs, An Economic Theory of Democracy 11–14 (1957).

9. Kenneth A. Shepsle & Mark S. Boncheck, Analyzing Politics: Rationality, Behavior and Institutions 115 (1997).

10. *See* James Fearon, *Electoral Accountability and the Control of Politicians: Selecting Good Types vs. Sanctioning Poor Performance, in* Democracy, Accountability and Representation 56 (Bernard Marin, Adam Przeworski, & Susan Stokes eds., 1999).

11. Harlow v. Fitzgerald, 457 U.S. 800 (1982).

12. *Id.* at 814.

13. *Id.*

14. U.S. Const. art. III §1.

15. U.S. Const. art. II §1.

16. The Federalist No. 79, at 472 (Alexander Hamilton) (Clinton Rossiter ed., 1961).

17. U.S. v. Hatter, 532 U.S. 557, 568 (2001) (Scalia, J., concurring) (quoting 1 James Kent, Commentaries on American Law *294 (1st ed. 1826)).

18. U.S. v. Will, 449 U.S. 200, 221 (1980).

19. *See,* e.g., Chief Justice William H. Rehnquist, 2000 Year-End Report on the Federal Judiciary (2001) (on file with the author); American Bar Association and Federal Bar Association, Federal Judicial Pay Erosion: A Report on the Need for Reform 15–17 (2001) (on file with the author).

20. U.S. Const. art. I, § 6.

21. 1 Max Farrand, Records of the Federal Convention of 1787 215 ("[Madison] observed that it would be improper to leave the members of the Natl. legislature to be provided for by the State Legisls: because it would create an improper dependence").

22. Joseph Story, Commentaries on the Constitution of the United States 2 §851 (1987).

23. Bernard Bailyn, The Ideological Origins of the American Revolution 46–51 (Enlarged Ed. 1992).

24. 1 Farrand, Records of the Federal Convention, *supra* note 21, at 426.

25. U.S. Const. art. I, §§2–3; U.S. Const. art. II, § 1.

26. U.S. Const. art. I, § 2; U.S. Const. amend. XII.

27. U.S. Const. art. II, § 2.

28. For an overview of relevant law, *see* Andrew Stark, Conflict of Interest in American Public Life (2000).

29. U.S. Const. art I. § 9, cl. 8 ("No Title of Nobility shall be granted by the United States: And no Person holding any Office of Profit or Trust under them, shall, without the Consent of the Congress, accept of any present, Emolument, Office, or Title, of any kind whatever, from any King, Prince or foreign State").

30. For introductions to the formal theory of screening, *see* Avinash Dixit & Susan Skeath, Games of Strategy 412 (1999); James D. Morrow, Game Theory for Political Scientists ch. 8 (1994). For an important application of screening mechanisms to political institutions, *see* Geoffrey Brennan & Alan Hamlin, Democratic Devices and Desires 72–76 (2000).

31. Thanks to Ed Iacobucci for this example. For a more complex example, *see* Geoffrey Brennan, *Selection and the Currency of Reward, in* THE THEORY OF INSTITUTIONAL DESIGN 256–274 (Robert E. Goodin ed., 1998).

32. Saul Levmore, *Precommitment Politics*, 82 VA. L. REV. 567 (1996). For an overview of conceptual and empirical issues, *see* Susan C. Stokes, MANDATES AND DEMOCRACY: NEOLIBERALISM BY SURPRISE IN LATIN AMERICA (2001).

33. 410 U.S. 113 (1973).

34. Elena Kagan, *Presidential Administration*, 114 HARV. L. REV. 2245, 2335 (2001).

35. David P. Currie, THE CONSTITUTION IN THE SUPREME COURT: THE SECOND CENTURY, 1888–1986 at 561 (1990).

36. *See* William N. Eskridge & John A. Ferejohn, *Super-Statutes*, 50 DUKE L.J. 1215, 1237 (2001).

37. *See* Alexander Keyssar, THE RIGHT TO VOTE: THE CONTESTED HISTORY OF DEMOCRACY IN THE UNITED STATES (2000).

38. It is logically possible that group X might be allowed to vote on all questions except revocation of its own voting rights, but I am unaware of any real-world examples.

39. On the trade-offs involved in districting, *see* Heather K. Gerken, *Second-Order Diversity*, 118 HARV. L. REV. 1099, 1117–1118 (2005).

40. *See* Robert D. Loevy, *Introduction: The Background and Setting of the Civil Rights Act of 1964, in* THE CIVIL RIGHTS ACT OF 1964: THE PASSAGE OF THE LAW THAT ENDED RACIAL SEGREGATION 3–40 (Robert D. Loevy, ed., 1997). For an overview of the Voting Rights Act's large effects on southern politics, *see* Richard H. Pildes, *The Politics of Race: Quiet Revolution in the South*, 108 HARV. L. REV. 1359 (1995).

41. U.S. CONST. art. I, §§2–3; U.S. CONST. art. II, § 1., *supra* note 25, and accompanying text.

42. U.S. Term Limits, Inc. v. Thornton, 514 U.S. 779 (1995).

43. *See* CONGRESSIONAL QUARTERLY'S GUIDE TO CONGRESS 560–561 (5th ed. 2000).

44. *See* U.S. CONST. amend. XXII.

45. *See* David Kyvig, EXPLICIT AND AUTHENTIC ACTS: AMENDING THE U.S. CONSTITUTION, 1776–1995 335 (1996) (discussing times when repeal was considered and stating, that this movement was "renewed momentarily after Richard Nixon's election to a second term in 1972 and Ronald Reagan's in 1984"); David Stout, *Assessing Clinton's Aspirations, Again*, N.Y. TIMES, May 30, 2003, at A24 (discussing Clinton's argument that

past presidents who have already served two terms should be eligible to serve as president again).

46. *GOP Senators Opt to Modify Terms for Chairmen; Six-Year Committee Rule Kept*, Washington Post, June 26, 2003, at A23.

47. *Dems Dump Chairmen Term Limits*, Politico, January 5, 2009, at http://www.politico.com/news/stories/0109/17100.html.

48. *See* Story, *supra* note 22.

49. *A Wise Ruling on Campus Fees*, N.Y. Times, March 24, 2000, at A20.

50. William Safire, *Free Speech v. Scalia*, N.Y. Times, April 29, 1985, at A17.

51. The best treatments of this are Lawrence Baum, The Puzzle of Judicial Behavior (1997) and Frederick Schauer, *Incentives, Reputation, and the Inglorious Determinants of Judicial Behavior*, 68 U. Cin. L. Rev. 615 (2000).

52. Jeffrey A. Segal & Albert D. Cover, *Ideological Values and the Votes of U.S. Supreme Court Justices*, 83 Am. Pol. Sci. Rev. 557 (1989). The standard assumption in the attitudinalist literature is that judicial preferences are stable over the course of the judicial career. For a contrary view, *see* Lee Epstein et al., *Do Judicial Preferences Change? A Longitudinal Study of U.S. Supreme Court Justices*, 60 J. Pol. 801 (1998).

53. *See* Segal & Cover, *supra* note 52.

54. William G. Ross, *Participation by the Public in the Federal Judicial Selection Process*, 43 Vand. L. Rev. 1, 3–5 (1990).

55. Richard A. Posner, The Federal Courts: Crisis and Reform 345–350 (1985).

56. United States v. Hatter, 532 U.S. 557, 568 (2001) (Scalia, J., concurring) (quoting Kent, *supra* note 17).

57. United States v. Will, 449 U.S. 200, 221 (1980).

58. *See* Michael J. Frank, *Judge Not, Lest You Be Judged Unworthy of a Pay Raise: An Examination of the Federal Judicial Salary "Crisis,"* 87 Marq. L. Rev. 55, 56 (2003) (noting that "these same salaries encourage veteran judges to seek the greener pastures of private law firms").

59. *See id.* ("The "paltry salaries of federal judicial officers are so insufficient that they discourage qualified attorneys from seeking federal judicial positions").

60. *See id.* (noting the increase in this point of view); Linda Greenhouse, *Pay Erodes, Judges Flee, & Relief is Not at Hand*, N.Y. Times, July 17, 2002, at A14.

61. *See* Daryl J. Levinson, *Empire-Building Government in Constitutional Law*, 118 Harv. L. Rev. 915, 923–937 (2005).

62. *Cf.* William H. Riker, *The Senate and American Federalism*, 49 A. POL. SCI. REV. 452, 469 (1955) ("by 1911, the state legislatures had lost all touch with national policy…[and] had been increasingly confined to the particular problems of their states").

63. *Introduction, in* POLITICAL EXTREMISM AND RATIONALITY xi–xxi (Albert Breton, Gianluigi Galeotti, Pierre Salmon, & Ronald Wintrobe, eds., 2002).

64. Juan Linz, THE BREAKDOWN OF DEMOCRATIC REGIMES: CRISIS, BREAKDOWN, AND REEQUILIBRATION 15 (1978).

65. *See id.* at 105 n. 6.

66. Luisa Giuriato & Maria Cristina Molinari, *Rationally Violent Tactics: Evidence from Modern Islamic Fundamentalism, in* POLITICAL EXTREMISM AND RATIONALITY 183–216 (Albert Breton, Gianluigi Galeotti, Pierre Salmon, & Ronald Wintrobe, eds., 2002).

67. Gitlow v. New York, 268 U.S. 652, 673 (1925) (Holmes, J., dissenting).

68. Geoffrey R. Stone, *Reflections on the First Amendment: The Evolution of the American Jurisprudence of Free Expression*, 131 PROCEED. AM. PHIL. SOC. 251 (1987).

69. John Finn, *Electoral Regimes and the Proscription of Anti-Democratic Parties, in* THE DEMOCRATIC EXPERIENCE AND POLITICAL VIOLENCE 51, 72 (David C. Rapoport & Leonard Weinberg, eds., 2001).

70. Brandenburg v. Ohio, 395 U.S. 444 (1969).

71. U.S. CONST. amend. XIV; Smith Act of 1940, 18 U.S.C. §2385 (2003).

72. Cass R. Sunstein, *Deliberative Trouble? Why Groups Go To Extremes*, 110 YALE L.J. 71 (2000).

73. *Cf.* Russell Hardin, *The Crippled Epistemology of Extremism, in* POLITICAL EXTREMISM AND RATIONALITY 3 (Albert Breton, Gianluigi Galeotti, Pierre Salmon, & Ronald Wintrobe, eds. 2002).

74. Adam Przeworski, CAPITALISM AND SOCIAL DEMOCRACY 35–38 (1985).

75. Barry R. Weingast, *Self-Enforcing Constitutions: With an Application to Democratic Stability in America's First Century*, March 2003 (unpublished manuscript available at http://lawweb.usc.edu/cslp/conferences/modeling_const_02/weingast.pdf).

76. See, e.g., Adam Przeworski, *Minimalist Conception of Democracy: A Defense, in* DEMOCRACY'S VALUE (Ian Shapiro and Casiano Hacker-Cordon, eds., 1999); Matthew C. Stephenson, *"When the Devil Turns…": The Political Foundations of Independent Judicial Review*, 32 J. LEGAL STUD. 59 (2003).

77. See Weingast, *supra* note 75, at 1–2.

78. This is a basic theme of Brennan & Hamlin, *supra* note 30.

CHAPTER 5

1. *See generally* Ronald Dworkin, Law's Empire (1986) [hereinafter Dworkin, Law's Empire].
2. *See* Ronald Dworkin, *In Praise of Theory*, 29 Ariz. St. L.J. 353, 364 (1997).
3. *See* Amartya Sen, *Rights and Agency*, 11 Phil. & Pub. Aff. 3, 3 (1982).
4. *See,* e.g., United States v. Taylor, 487 U.S. 326, 346 (1988) (Scalia, J., concurring in part) ("[W]e have an obligation to conduct our exegesis in a fashion which fosters th[e] democratic process [specified in the bicameralism and presentment requirements of Article I]"); Elizabeth Garrett, *Legal Scholarship in the Age of Legislation*, 34 Tulsa L.J. 679, 685 (1999) ("[M]ethods like textualism and rules of clear statement are best understood as efforts to improve the quality of the decisionmaking in the politically accountable branches"); *cf.* W. David Slawson, *Legislative History and the Need To Bring Statutory Interpretation Under the Rule of Law*, 44 Stan. L. Rev. 383, 407–410 (1992) (arguing that judicial recourse to legislative history results in irresponsible and incoherent congressional lawmaking).
5. For discussion of this issue, see Einer Elhauge, Statutory Default Rules 332–334 (2008).
6. *See* Elhauge, *supra* note 5, at 333.
7. *See* David A. Strauss, *Common Law, Common Ground, and Jefferson's Principle*, 112 Yale L.J. 1717, 1730–1731 (2003).
8. *See* Erin O'Hara, *Social Constraint or Implicit Collusion?: Toward a Game Theoretic Analysis of Stare Decisis*, 24 Seton Hall L. Rev. 736, 748–753 (1993).
9. This distinction is slightly inaccurate. Although a one-shot Prisoners' Dilemma has no coordination element—each player has a dominant strategy—a repeated version of the game makes coordination important. *See* O'Hara, *supra* note 8, at 751–753. The difference is that games such as Assurance have coordination built into their very structure. See Richard H. McAdams, *Beyond the Prisoners' Dilemma: Coordination, Game Theory, and Law*, 82 S. Cal. L. Rev. 209, 220–222 (2009).
10. *See* McAdams, *supra* note 9, at 222–223; *cf.* Strauss, *supra* note 7, at 1733–1735. For hybrid games in which the Battle of the Sexes is embedded within an iterated Prisoners' Dilemma, see McAdams, *supra* note 9, at 226–230. Such refinements, while important, are not necessary for the points I attempt to make here.

11. *See* James D. Morrow, GAME THEORY FOR POLITICAL SCIENTISTS 95 (1994).
12. In previous work, I failed to take adequate account of this problem for Thayerians. See, for example, the brief and unsatisfactory remarks in Adrian Vermeule, JUDGING UNDER UNCERTAINTY: AN INSTITUTIONAL THEORY OF LEGAL INTERPRETATION 263–264 (2006). For suggestions that the Court should eliminate judicial review only prospectively, and that unilateral disarmament is a bad idea, see Mark Tushnet, TAKING THE CONSTITUTION AWAY FROM THE COURTS 175 (1999).
13. Tushnet, *supra* note 12, at 57–65.
14. For a systemic analysis of the marginal effects and interdependencies of cumulating safeguards of federalism, see Jenna Bednar, THE ROBUST FEDERATION (2009) chapter 7 passim.
15. For more on the problem of local maxima, see generally Jon Elster, EXPLAINING SOCIAL BEHAVIOR: MORE NUTS AND BOLTS FOR THE SOCIAL SCIENCES 111, 248–249 (2007).
16. Cass R. Sunstein, *Incompletely Theorized Agreements*, 108 HARV. L. REV. 1733 (1995).
17. Cass R. Sunstein, RADICALS IN ROBES 27–30 (2005).
18. The issue is slightly complicated by a putative distinction between interpretation and adjudication. Some originalists believe that this distinction is coherent, and that originalism is the only valid form of interpretation, whereas originalism as a method of adjudication must be justified by reference to its consequences. See, e.g., Gary Lawson, Response, *On Reading Recipes... and Constitutions*, 85 GEO. L.J. 1823, 1823–1824 (1997). Other originalists do not seem to draw such a distinction, saying generally that "originalism" has pragmatic benefits. *See, e.g.,* John O. McGinnis & Michael B. Rappaport, *A Pragmatic Defense of Originalism*, 31 HARV. J.L. & PUB. POL'Y 917 (2008) [hereinafter McGinnis & Rappaport, *A Pragmatic Defense of Originalism*]. I will confine my remarks to originalist adjudication and so will ignore the issue here.
19. Posting of Randy Barnett to Legal Affairs Debate Club: Constitution in Exile?, http://legalaffairs.org/webexclusive/debateclub_cie0505.msp (May 3, 2005, 13:43), *quoted in* Cass R. Sunstein, *Of Snakes and Butterflies: A Reply*, 106 COLUM. L. REV. 2234, 2236 & n. 8 (2006) (book review).
20. *See* Jonathan R. Macey, *Originalism as an "Ism,"* 19 HARV. J.L. & PUB. POL'Y 301, 303–304 (1996).

21. *See generally* Bruce Ackerman, WE THE PEOPLE: FOUNDATIONS (1991).

22. *See generally* McGinnis & Rappaport, *A Pragmatic Defense of Originalism,* *supra* note 18; John O. McGinnis and Michael D. Rappaport, *Originalism and the Good Constitution,* 98 GEO. L.J. 1693 (2010) [hereinafter McGinnis and Rappaport, *Originalism and the Good Constitution*].

23. *See generally* Robert H. Bork, THE TEMPTING OF AMERICA (1990).

24. Larry Kramer, *Two (More) Problems with Originalism,* 31 HARV. J.L. & PUB. POL'Y 907, 915 (2008); *see also* Lawrence Lessig, *Fidelity in Translation,* 71 TEX. L. REV. 1165, 1182–1188 (1993).

25. Lessig, *Fidelity in Translation, supra* note 24, at 1189–1192.

26. Antonin Scalia, *Originalism: The Lesser Evil,* 57 U. CIN. L. REV. 849, 864 (1989).

27. *See* Randy E. Barnett, *Trumping Precedent with Original Meaning: Not as Radical as It Sounds,* 22 CONST. COMMENT. 257, 263–269 (2005). I have compressed two of Barnett's categories—"construction" and "liquidation"—into one, because they largely overlap.

28. *See id.* at 269–270 (arguing that this version of originalism leaves ample room for the doctrine of precedent).

29. 272 U.S. 52 (1926).

30. *See id.* at 176.

31. 295 U.S. 602 (1935).

32. *Id.* at 626 (limiting *Myers* to very narrow factual circumstances despite the *Myers* Court's extensive historical analysis).

33. For a consequentialist theory that attempts to square originalism and precedent, see John O. McGinnis & Michael B. Rappaport, *Reconciling Originalism and Precedent,* 103 NW. U. L. REV. 803 (2009). In my view, the attempt fails to cope with precedents like *Humphrey's Executor.* See id. at n. 173 (conceding that the precedents creating independent agencies would be indefensible on their theory, but making an arbitrary exception for the independent Federal Reserve).

34. According to a recent review of the evidence, "it is a mistake to characterize the justices on the Court as strategic actors, who take advantage of their strategic positions to achieve their legal or policy goals. Strategic behavior occurs on the Court, but it takes place much less often than the strategic scholars claim." Saul Brenner & Joseph M. Whitmeyer, STRATEGY ON THE UNITED STATES SUPREME COURT 165 (2009).

35. For clear statements that these two axes are distinct, see Lee Epstein and Tonja Jacobi, *The Strategic Analysis of Judicial Decisions,* 6 ANNU. REV. L. SOC. SCI. 341, 344 (2010); Lawrence Baum, JUDGES AND THEIR

AUDIENCES: A PERSPECTIVE ON JUDICIAL BEHAVIOR 6–8 (2006). "[I]n most strategic models that are applied to federal courts, judges act solely on the goal of achieving good policy," *id.* at 6, but as Baum points out, there is no logical connection between assuming that judges are strategic and assuming that they are attitudinal, in the sense of policy-oriented, rather than legalist, *see id.* at 7–8. Some of the literature states that judges are "single-minded seekers of *legal policy.*" Tracey E. George & Lee Epstein, *On the Nature of Supreme Court Decision Making*, 86 AM. POL. SCI. REV. 323, 325 (1992) (emphasis added). However, this formulation is intrinsically ambiguous.

36. *See generally* Jeffrey A. Segal & Harold J. Spaeth, THE SUPREME COURT AND THE ATTITUDINAL MODEL REVISITED (2002).

37. *See generally* Lee Epstein & Jack Knight, THE CHOICES JUSTICES MAKE (1998).

38. There is only a small body of work that models judges as strategic maximizers of their legal views. *See, e.g.,* John A. Ferejohn & Barry R. Weingast, *A Positive Theory of Statutory Interpretation*, 12 INT'L REV. L. & ECON. 263, 268 (1992) (using the phrase "politically sophisticated honest agent" to describe strategic legalism as one of three models of judicial interpretation); Gregory Sisk et al., *Charting the Influences on the Judicial Mind: An Empirical Study of Judicial Reasoning*, 73 N.Y.U. L. REV. 1377 (1988). For a hybrid argument that strategic judges advance their views of both good law and good policy, see Pablo T. Spiller & Emerson H. Tiller, *Invitations to Override: Congressional Reversals of Supreme Court Decisions*, 16 INT'L REV. L. & ECON. 503, 504 (1996).

39. Thanks to Daryl Levinson for suggesting this term.

40. On this sort of paradoxical structure, in which certain states of affairs cannot be attained by an agent who wishes to attain them, but can only arise as a by-product, see Jon Elster, SOUR GRAPES: STUDIES IN THE SUBVERSION OF RATIONALITY (1985).

41. *See, e.g.,* Gonzales v. Raich, 545 U.S. 1, 58 (2005) (Thomas, J., dissenting) (rejecting the Court's understanding of the Commerce Clause in favor of an understanding based on the "text, structure, and history" of the clause); Whitman v. Am. Trucking Ass'n, 531 U.S. 457, 487 (2001) (Thomas, J., concurring) (questioning the Court's reliance on the intelligible principle doctrine in delegation jurisprudence). Cf. McGinnis and Rappaport, *Originalism and the Good Constitution, supra* note 22, at 1750 (arguing that "departing from originalism undermines its public attractiveness and makes it difficult to generate a legal culture of originalism").

42. *See* McAdams, *supra* note 9, at 212–213.

43. Jon Elster quotes a dictum of Montaigne's: "In the state of indecision and perplexity brought upon us by our inability to see what is most advantageous and to choose it…, since we doubt which is the shorter road, we should keep going straight ahead." Jon Elster, *Mimicking Impartiality, in* JUSTICE AND DEMOCRACY 112, 113 (Keith Dowding, Robert E. Goodin & Carole Pateman eds., 2004) (quoting MICHEL E. DE MONTAIGNE, ESSAYS 144 (M.A. Screech trans., 1992)).

44. McGinnis and Rappaport, *Originalism and the Good Constitution, supra* note 22, at 1748–1752, seems to offer an argument with this structure.

45. Scott E. Page, DIVERSITY AND COMPLEXITY 183–195 (2011).

46. Krishna K. Ladha, *The Condorcet Jury Theorem, Free Speech, and Correlated Votes,* 36 Am. J. POL. SCI. 617, 625–630 (1992). For an extensive treatment, see generally Scott E. Page, THE DIFFERENCE: HOW THE POWER OF DIVERSITY CREATES BETTER GROUPS, FIRMS, SCHOOLS, AND SOCIETIES (2007).

47. Cass R. Sunstein, WHY SOCIETIES NEED DISSENT 111–144 (2003). *See generally* Cass R. Sunstein, GOING TO EXTREMES: HOW LIKE MINDS UNITE AND DIVIDE (2009).

48. *See* Sunstein, WHY SOCIETIES NEED DISSENT, *supra* note 47, at 112–114.

49. Cf. Cass R. Sunstein, David Schkade, and Lisa Michelle Ellman, *Ideological Voting on the Federal Courts of Appeals: A Preliminary Investigation,* 90 VA. L. REV. 301 (2004).

50. *See, e.g.,* Morrison v. Olson, 487 U.S. 654, 697–734 (1988) (Scalia, J., dissenting).

51. *See, e.g.,* INS v. Chadha, 462 U.S. 919, 967–1003 (1983) (White, J., dissenting).

52. United States v. Nixon, 418 U.S. 683, 707 (1974).

53. 487 U.S. 654 (1988).

54. 524 U.S. 417 (1998).

55. *See id.* at 466–469 (Scalia, J., concurring in part and dissenting in part).

56. *See id.* at 476 (Breyer, J., dissenting).

57. *See* Thomas O. Sargentich, *The Contemporary Debate About Legislative-Executive Separation of Powers,* 72 CORNELL L. REV. 430, 486 (1987).

58. *See* Frederick Schauer, *A Critical Guide to Vehicles in the Park,* 83 N.Y.U. L. REV. 1109, 1127–1129 (2008); Frederick Schauer, *The Practice and Problems of Plain Meaning: A Response to Aleinikoff and Shaw,* 45 VAND. L. REV. 715, 729 (1992).

59. *See* Cernauskas v. Fletcher, 201 S.W.2d 999, 1000 (Ark. 1947).

60. Church of the Holy Trinity v. United States, 143 U.S. 457 (1892).

61. *Id.* at 458–462. For an argument that *Holy Trinity* got the legislative intentions and purposes wrong, thus creating rather than avoiding a mistake, see Adrian Vermeule, *Legislative History and the Limits of Judicial Competence: The Untold Story of* Holy Trinity Church, 50 STAN. L. REV. 1833 (1998). For a contrasting view, see Carol Chomsky, *Unlocking the Mysteries of* Holy Trinity: *Spirit, Letter, and History in Statutory Interpretation,* 100 COLUM. L. REV. 901 (2000).

62. Dworkin, LAW'S EMPIRE, *supra* note 1.

CONCLUSION

1. *See* Daryl J. Levinson, *Empire-Building Government in Constitutional Law,* 118 HARV. L. REV. 915, 923–937 (2005).

2. See the sources cited in the introduction.

3. *See* Frederick A. Schauer, *On the Nature of the Nature of Law* (unpublished manuscript, available at http://papers.ssrn.com/sol3/papers.cfm?abstract_id=1836494).

4. *See* Ronald Dworkin, LAW'S EMPIRE (1986).

5. As political scientists, to their credit, have recognized. *See,* e.g., Jeffrey R. Lax, *The New Judicial Politics of Legal Doctrine,* 14 ANNU. REV. POLIT. SCI. 131, 137 (2011), and sources cited therein.

INDEX

actors. *See* constitutional actors
adversarial system of litigation
   arguments for, 69, 72, 187n74
   critiques of, 69, 82
   dilemma of second best in, 91–93,
      199n84
   truth-finding in, 35, 69, 82, 91–92,
      94–95, 98, 187n74
aggregate systems
   constitutional orders as, 3, 5, 23, 27, 175
   members of, 16, 23–27
   one-level systems, 27
   two-level systems, 3, 5, 23, 27–29, 175
      See also aggregation; constitutional
      orders; system effects
aggregation
   of beliefs and judgments, 19, 27, 47, 70
   miracle of, 19–21, 46
   miracle of judicial, 22, 58–60, 171,
      192n76, 192n79
   nightmare of, 60, 61
   of preferences, 18–19
   surprising consequences of, 5, 8, 97
      See also systems theory
amendments to Constitution. *See* U.S.
      Constitutional Amendments
arbitrary stopping rules, 19, 27, 28
Arrow, Kenneth
   on norms, 84–85, 86
      See also Arrow's Theorem

Arrow's Theorem, 19, 23, 27–28, 175
Ascertainment Clause, 108–110, 111, 113,
   121, 202n21
Assurance Game, 94, 142–143, 199n86,
   206n9

Beard, Charles, 46
bicameralism. *See* legislatures
Bickel, Alexander
   contest theory of free speech, 68,
      83–84, 94–95
   on "countermajoritarian difficulty," 55
Boumediene v. Bush, 57
British Crown. *See* divide-and-conquer tactics
Bryce, James, 20
Burkean judges, 135, 141–144

capitalism. *See* economic theory
checks and balances. *See* Madisonian checks
      and balances; separation of powers
Clinton v. City of New York, 166
Coase theorem, 67, 75, 76
collective action
   democracy-forcing efforts by
      judiciary, 139
   described, 17
   free-rider problem in, 17, 18
   in Madisonian checks and balances, 41
   malign vs. benign outcomes, 18
   and public welfare, 17–18

commerce power. *See* legislatures
common law
   and economic performance, 200*n*101
   invisible-hand mechanisms in, 69, 71, 72
   truth-gathering in, 98, 99
Communism, 98, 128, 130
Compensation Clause, 106–108, 111,
   113, 123–125, 204*n*58–59
compensation for officeholders
   monetary, 106–110, 111, 121,
     123–125, 132–133
   nonpecuniary, 112–113, 133, 202*n*29
   See also Ascertainment Clause;
     Compensation Clause
Condorcet's Jury Theorem. *See* Jury Theorem
Condorcet's voting paradox, 14, 18–19, 27
   See also Arrow's Theorem
Congress
   and committee term limits, 120–121
   as representative of nation, 47, 52
   See also legislatures
consequentialism, 135, 136–137
Constitution. *See* structural constitution;
   U.S. Constitution
constitutional actors
   problems of second best for, 10
   pros and cons of system awareness, 6,
     7, 36–37, 46, 176
   See also judicial system; legislatures;
     presidency
constitutional analysis
   importance of systemic perspective,
     3–7, 8, 10, 175–178
   long-term vs. short-term, 131–132
   and system effects, 5, 36, 37, 38,
     187*n*79
   See also constitutional judging;
     invisible-hand justifications; second
     best perspectives; selection effects
constitutional judging
   advantages of systemic perspective, 6,
     7, 10, 11–13, 134–136, 168–174,
     173–174
   Burkeans, 135, 141–144
   costs/benefits of methodological
     diversity, 135, 161–168, 171–172
   democracy-forcing approaches, 138–141

   evangelism in, 156–157
   ideal types of judges, 154–155
   interdependency in, 7, 11–12
   and judicial appointments, 13,
     171–172, 174
   and judicial homogeneity, 172–173
   and legal chameleons, 13, 160–161,
     167, 170–172
   and limited judicial capacities, 156, 157–160
   minimalists in a maximalist
     world, 148–149
   originalism, 7, 35, 135, 136, 149–153,
     158, 207*n*18
   principled consequentialism, 12, 135,
     136–137
   role of precedent in, 135, 141–144
   and second-best adjudication, 12, 35,
     137–138, 172–173
   and strategic legalism, 12–13,
     134–135, 153–156, 169, 206*n*4,
     208*n*34–35, 209*n*38
   and strategic naïveté, 7, 156–160, 169,
     210*n*43
   textualism, 12, 138
   Thayerism, 12, 135, 144–148, 149
   See also U.S. Supreme Court
constitutional orders
   as aggregate systems, 3, 5, 23, 27, 175
   fallacy of composition for, 15, 50
   member types in, 23–24
   problems of second best in, 10
   system effects in, 14–15
   two main features of American, 52
   See also constitutional analysis;
     constitutional judging;
     constitutional rules
constitutional rules
   commerce and enumeration, 125–127
   as self-stabilizing, 11, 102, 117–123
   as self-undermining, 11, 102, 123–131
   systemic feedback from, 11, 101–102,
     116–117, 131, 133
   tolerance for intolerant, 127–131
   See also Ascertainment Clause;
     Compensation Clause; free press;
     free speech; officeholders; selection
     effects; voting rights

constitutional structure. *See* structural
  constitution
Contracts Clause, 117
countermajoritarian difficulty, 55–58
criminal procedure
  analogy to markets, 68, 73–75
  and invisible-hand arguments, 65, 68–69, 72
  and rule of lenity, 138
  See also adversarial system of litigation;
    inquisitorial system of litigation

Dahl, Robert, 50
democracy
  emergent, 50–54
  equating with majoritarianism, 50
  and proscription of antidemocratic
    parties, 129–131
Demsetz, Harold, 69–70, 75
diachronic system effects. *See* system effects
discursive dilemma, 22–23
divide-and-conquer tactics, 31, 43–46,
    189n19, 189n22
doctrinal paradox, 14, 22–23
Dworkin, Ronald, 136, 169, 177

economic theory
  and norms, 81, 82–83
  and paradox of thrift, 17–18, 183n12
  and role of incentives, 11
  and theory of second best, 9, 30
  Tragedy of the Commons, 17, 71–72
  See also Hayek, Friedrich; markets;
    Smith, Adam
elections
  and miracle of aggregation, 19–21, 46
  selection effects of, 102–104, 201n5
  system effects in, 46–48, 189n31
  See also Electoral College
Electoral College, 47, 50, 51
Elster, Jon, 185n54, 186n57, 188n10,
    196n48, 198n72–73, 207n15,
    209n40, 210n43
Ely, John Hart, 56
emergent properties of groups
  defined, 182n6
  production of, 8, 9
  See also systems theory

English common law, 32
epistemic accuracy, 161–162
Equal Rights Amendment, 24–25
executive. *See* presidency

fallacy of composition
  defined, 9
  examples of, 15, 16, 17, 18, 19–20,
    26–27, 28, 30, 39, 41, 44–45, 46, 47,
    48, 50, 54, 55–56, 97, 145–146,
    160, 178
fallacy of division
  defined, 9
  examples of, 15, 16, 17, 21–22, 30, 39,
    50, 55, 57, 63, 98, 134–135, 137, 139,
    150, 155–156, 159–160, 176
fascism, 128, 129
Ferguson, Adam, 39
Fifteenth Amendment, 118, 119
formalism, 165, 166–168
Fourteenth Amendment, 25
free markets. *See* markets
free press, 121–123
free speech
  Bickel's contest theory of, 68, 83–84,
    94–95
  increasing importance over time, 117
  invisible-hand arguments for, 65, 68
  and media, 90
  relevant good arising from, 72
  as self-stabilizing rule, 121–123
  and theory of second best, 90
  and World War II, 97
French monarchy, 31
functionalism, 165–166, 167, 168

Germany, 129
gerrymandering, 53
Gulick, Luther, 97

Hamilton, Alexander, 107
Hayek, Friedrich
  argument for explicit markets, 67, 72
  on competition as discovery
    procedure, 66, 95–96, 97–98, 200n91
Hercules (mythical judge), 169, 177
Hewlett-Packard, 71, 79

Hitler, Adolf, 128
Holmes, Oliver Wendell, Jr., 68, 72, 128
Holy Trinity case, 168
Hume, David
  on British divide-and-conquer
    tactics, 31, 43–46
  on hereditary monarchies, 31, 186n59
  "knavery principle," 103
  and Scottish Enlightenment, 39
  use of invisible-hand reasoning, 39
Humphrey's Executor v. United States, 153, 208n33

immunity, selection effects of, 104–106, 111
inquisitorial system of litigation, 34–35, 98,
    187n74
invisible-hand justifications
  common elements of, 70–80, 195n21
  defined, 10–11, 16
  diachronic vs. synchronic, 71
  dilemma of norms, 66, 80–87, 100,
    197n66–67
  dilemma of second best, 66, 82, 87–94,
    100, 198n71
  dilemma of verification, 66–67, 73,
    94–99, 100
  malign vs. benign outcomes, 16
  prominent examples of, 67–70
  as tool of systemic analysis, 10–11, 65,
    99–100
  See also Madisonian checks and
    balances; Smith, Adam
Italian Fascists, 129

judicial appointments, 13, 171–172
judicial biases
  and miracle of aggregation, 22, 58–60,
    171, 192n76, 192n79
  and New Legal Realism, 59, 63
  and nightmare of aggregation, 60, 61
  system effects of, 4, 6, 15, 58–63, 172,
    193n83, 193n85
  See also constitutional judging
judicial system
  interdependency in, 7, 11–12
  See also constitutional judging; judicial
    appointments; judicial biases; U.S.
    Supreme Court

Jury Theorem
  and accuracy in large groups, 21–22, 70,
    161–162, 169
  description, 15–16, 183n21

Kennedy, Anthony, 60–61, 192n80
Keynes, John Maynard, 183n12

Landis, James, 33–34
legal chameleons. *See* constitutional judging
legal theory
  and ethical norms, 81–82
  formalism and functionalism, 165–167
  and role of incentives, 11
  systemic perspective on, 6, 7, 8–9, 38,
    168–169, 176
  and theory of second best, 30–32, 91–93
  See also adversarial system of litigation;
    inquisitorial system of litigation;
    judicial system
legislatures
  and bicameralism, 28–29, 48–49
  and Coasean bargaining, 76–77
  and intentionalism, 139–140
  and legislative aggrandizement,
    125–127, 205n62
  on mutability of laws, 31–32, 186n60
  and preference cycling, 28
  system effects in, 10, 43–49
  vote-buying and divide-and-conquer
    strategy, 43–46, 189n19, 189n22
  See also elections
Levinson, Sanford, 50
List, Christian, 22, 182n5–6, 184n27
litigation. *See* adversarial system of
    litigation; inquisitorial system of
    litigation
Luhmann, Niklas, 181n3

Madisonian checks and balances
  and executive power, 33–34
  flaws in, 40–43
  influence of Adam Smith on, 17, 39, 42,
    67, 75
  invisible-hand reasoning
    underpinning, 39, 40, 42, 65, 67, 71,
    75–76

property rights, and invisible hand, 65,
  69–70, 71, 75
proscription laws, 129–131

Rehnquist, William, 165–166
Roman constitution, 30–31
Roosevelt Court, 144
Roosevelt, Franklin D., 120

Scalia, Antonin, 35, 158, 206n4
Scottish Enlightenment, 17, 39, 67, 75
  See also Hume, David; Smith, Adam
second best perspectives
  in adversarial system of litigation,
    91–93, 199n84
  in constitutional analysis/theory, 10,
    12, 32–35, 36, 37
  dilemma of, 66, 82, 87–94, 100, 198n71
  and invisible-hand justifications, 66, 82,
    87–94, 100, 198n71
  and norms, 82, 87
  and political parties, 89–90, 198n78
  in political theory, 9, 30–32, 89–90
  relationship to system effects, 9–10,
    29–35, 87
  and separation of powers, 90–91, 93–94
  theory of, 29–30
  See also constitutional judging
selection analysis
  and compensation for
    officeholders, 132–133
  and heterogeneous candidate
    pools, 132
  and long-term vs. short-term
    constitutional analysis, 131–132
  as tool for examining diachronic
    constitutional change, 101–102, 131
  See also selection effects
selection effects
  of Ascertainment Clause, 108–110,
    111, 113, 121, 202n21
  and causal aftereffects, 115–116
  of Compensation Clauses, 106–108,
    111, 113, 123–125, 204n58–59
  direct vs. indirect, 111–116
  as driver of constitutional change, 11,
    101–102, 116–117

of elections, 102–104, 201n5
of incentives and compensation,
    106–110, 111, 112–113, 121,
    202n29
of official immunity, 104–106, 111
of screening mechanisms, 114–115
selection of whom by whom, 110–111
of self-stabilizing constitutional
    rules, 118–123
of self-undermining constitutional
    rules, 123–131
systemic feedback from, 11, 101–102,
    116–117, 131, 133, 201n1
  See also constitutional rules
Senate, 50, 51
separation of powers
  bargaining in, 67, 76–77, 78
  dilemma of second best in, 90–91,
    93–94
  formalism and functionalism in, 165–167
  invisible hand underpinning, 65
  relevant good arising from, 77–78,
    196n45
  See also Madisonian checks and balances
Smith, Adam
  influence on Madisonian constitutional
    design, 17, 39, 42, 75
  invisible-hand reasoning of, 39, 42, 67,
    193n1
  on markets, 17, 42, 67
  on pricing, 85
  See also markets
Stephen, James Fitzjames, 32, 68–69, 72,
    187n74
Story, Joseph, 108
strategic legalism. *See* constitutional judging
Strauss, David, 24–26
structural constitution
  calls for reform of, 50, 54–55
  and countermajoritarian difficulty,
    55–58
  defined, 10
  and emergent democracy, 50–55
  invisible-hand reasoning central to, 39,
    40, 42, 65, 67
  and judicial system, 58–63
  legislature-executive interactions, 43–49

systems level approach to, 10,
  38–64, 100
See also judicial system; legislatures;
  Madisonian checks and balances;
  presidency; U.S. Constitution
Supreme Court. *See* U.S. Supreme Court
synchronic system effects. *See* system
  effects
system effects
  in constitutional analysis/theory, 5–6,
    36, 37, 187*n*79
  defined, 14, 15–16
  diachronic vs. synchronic, 11, 71, 101
  in elections, 46–48, 189*n*31
  examples of, 14
  of judicial biases, 4, 6, 58–63, 172,
    193*n*83, 193*n*85
  in one-level systems, 16–23
  pitfalls of overlooking, 9, 15
  in propositions, 23–26
  of structural constitution, 10,
    38–64, 100
  surprise consequences of, 5, 7, 8
  and theory of second best, 9–10,
    29–35, 87
  in two-level systems, 27–29
  See also aggregation; collective action;
    doctrinal paradox; invisible-hand
    justifications; Jury Theorem;
    Madisonian checks and balances;
    structural constitution
systemic analysis/perspective
  incentive analysis vs. selection
    analysis, 101–102, 131–133
  promise and limitations of, 6, 36–37, 176
  two crucial tools of, 10–11
  See also constitutional analysis;
    constitutional judging; invisible-hand
    justifications; selection effects;
    structural constitution; systems theory
systems
  defined, 3
  See also aggregates; systemic analysis/
    perspectives; systems theory
systems theory
  application across multiple fields, 8,
    181*n*3

core ideas of, 8–9, 181*n*4, 182*n*6
pseudoscience surrounding, 8
See also system effects; systemic
  analysis/perspective

Take Care Clause, 153
term limits
  Congressional committees, 120–121
  for presidency, 120, 203*n*45
textualism, 12, 138
Thayerism, 12, 135, 144–148, 149
Thayer, James Bradley, 12
Thomas, Clarence, 157
Tocqueville, Alexis de, 31
tolerance. *See* constitutional rules
Tragedy of the Commons, 17, 71–72
Twenty-fourth Amendment, 25
Twenty-second Amendment, 120

Ullmann-Margalit, Edna, 70, 78
U.S. Constitution
  calls for reform of, 50, 54–55
  Contracts Clause, 117
  as democratic, 50
  Take Care Clause, 153
  Vesting Clause, 153
  See also Ascertainment Clause;
    Compensation Clause; constitutional
    analysis; constitutional judging; free
    speech; Madisonian checks and
    balances; structural constitution
U.S. Constitutional Amendments
  Fifteenth Amendment, 118, 119
  Fourteenth Amendment, 25
  irrelevance arguments about, 24–27
  Nineteenth Amendment, 25, 118
  proposed Child Labor Amendment, 26
  proposed Equal Rights
    Amendment, 24–25
  Twenty-fourth Amendment, 25
  Twenty-second Amendment, 120
U.S. Supreme Court
  Boumediene v. Bush, 57
  Clinton v. City of New York, 166
  and countermajoritarian difficulty,
    55–58
  current court, 60–61

U.S. Supreme Court (*continued*)
    debates about democracy of, 50, 51–52
    and free speech rulings, 121–123
    Humphrey's Executor v. United
        States, 153, 208*n*33
    and ideological attitudes at
        nomination, 122–123, 204*n*52
    invalidation of executive action
        by, 57–58
    and judicial miracle of aggregation, 22,
        58–60, 171, 192*n*76, 192*n*79
    models of preference cycling, 27, 28,
        184*n*42, 185*n*46
    Morrison v. Olson, 166

Myers v. United States, 153
nightmare of aggregation, 60, 61
Roosevelt Court, 144
Warren Court, 144
See also constitutional judging; judicial
    biases; judicial system

Vesting Clause, 153
vote-buying, 43–46, 189*n*19, 189*n*22
voting paradox, 14, 18–19
voting rights, 118–119, 203*n*38
Voting Rights Act of 1965, 110, 118, 119

White, Byron, 165–166

Lightning Source UK Ltd.
Milton Keynes UK
UKHW010307041022
409889UK00002B/38